Cell Phones in the Classroom

A Practical Guide for Educators

Liz Kolb

International Society for Technology in Education

EUGENE, OREGON ▪ WASHINGTON, DC

Cell Phones in the Classroom
A Practical Guide for Educators

Liz Kolb

Director of Book Publishing: *Courtney Burkholder*
Acquisitions Editor: *Jeff V. Bolkan*
Production Editors: *Lynda Gansel, Tina Wells*
Production Coordinator: *Rachel Williams*
Graphic Designer: *Signe Landin*
Copy Editor: *Kristin Landon*
Proofreader: *Katherine Gries*
Book/Cover Design and Production: *Sandy Kupsch*

SUSTAINABLE FORESTRY INITIATIVE — Label applies to the text stock
Certified Fiber Sourcing
www.sfiprogram.org

Library of Congress Cataloging-in-Publication Data
Kolb, Liz.
  Cell phones in the classroom : a practical guide for educators / Liz Kolb. — 1st ed.
    p. cm.
  ISBN 978-1-56484-299-2 (pbk.)
  1. Educational technology—United States—Case studies. 2. Telephone in education—United States—Case studies. 3. Cell phones—United States—Case studies. I. Title.
  LB1028.3.K647 2011
  371.33—dc22

                                          2011011795

First Edition
ISBN: 978-1-56484-299-2
Printed in the United States of America

About ISTE

The International Society for Technology in Education (ISTE) is the trusted source for professional development, knowledge generation, advocacy, and leadership for innovation. ISTE is the premier membership association for educators and education leaders engaged in improving teaching and learning by advancing the effective use of technology in PK–12 and teacher education.

Home of the National Educational Technology Standards (NETS) and ISTE's annual conference and exposition (formerly known as NECC), ISTE represents more than 100,000 professionals worldwide. We support our members with information, networking opportunities, and guidance as they face the challenge of transforming education. To find out more about these and other ISTE initiatives, visit our website at www.iste.org.

As part of our mission, ISTE Book Publishing works with experienced educators to develop and produce practical resources for classroom teachers, teacher educators, and technology leaders. Every manuscript we select for publication is carefully peer-reviewed and professionally edited. We value your feedback on this book and other ISTE products. Email us at books@iste.org.

International Society for Technology in Education (ISTE)
Washington, DC, Office:
  1710 Rhode Island Ave. NW, Suite 900, Washington, DC 20036-3132
Eugene, Oregon, Office:
  180 West 8th Ave., Suite 300, Eugene, OR 97401-2916
Order Desk: 1.800.336.5191
Order Fax: 1.541.302.3778
Customer Service: orders@iste.org
Book Publishing: books@iste.org
Book Sales and Marketing: booksmarketing@iste.org
Web: www.iste.org

About the Author

Liz Kolb is the author of *Toys to Tools: Connecting Student Cell Phones to Education*, as well as numerous articles for ISTE's *Learning & Leading with Technology*. She has a PhD in learning technologies from the University of Michigan as well as a master's degree in curriculum and instruction from Ashland University. She is currently an adjunct assistant professor at Madonna University in Livonia, Michigan, and a lecturer and research associate at the University of Michigan. Liz works with inservice and preservice teachers on teaching 21st century-technology education. She has done workshops, webinars, and inservices throughout the United States. Liz also spent seven years as a secondary teacher in Ohio. She taught social studies and computer technology courses. In addition she spent four years as a high school technology coordinator in Columbus Ohio. Liz resides in Ann Arbor, Michigan.

Acknowledgments

This book would not have been possible without selfless participation from 17 inspiring educators: Tim Chase, Stephen Collis, Carla Dolman, Andrew Douch, Jimbo Lamb, Larry Liu, Judy Pederson, Alison Riccardi, Rebekah Randall, Jarrod Robinson, Kipp Rogers, Lynne Sullivan, Katie Titler, Toni Twiss, Rick Weinberg, Kathy Tevington, and Paul Wood. There were many teachers, student teachers, and educators in my personal learning network who inspired me with their ideas as I worked on this book. I must thank everyone at ISTE; they have continued to believe in my work and have given me a forum to share what teachers are doing with student cell phones. Thanks in particular to Jeff Bolkan, who gave me the inspiration for writing this book. I'd also like to thank my father, a wonderful teacher in his own right, who spent many tireless hours editing this book.

I could write an entire book about the numerous friends, family, and colleagues who have supported and guided me during the last two years of putting this book together. I wish I had the writing space to name each one of you.

Dedication

For B … 100%

Contents

Chapter 3
Cell Phone Use for School Administration

Chapter 4
Sample Lesson Plans and Tutorials

Chapter 5

Getting Started

Chapter 6

Web 2.0 Tools That Couple with Cell Phones

Introduction

This book is a follow-up to my 2008 book, *Toys to Tools: Using Student Cell Phones in Education*. When I wrote the first book (between 2005 and 2007), I knew of only four K–12 teachers in the United States who had tried using students' cell phones as learning tools. However, I was aware of the great number of middle and high school students who owned cell phones. Therefore, I focused on the possibilities of how cell phones could be used to extend secondary school learning outside of the classroom. That book explored lesson ideas, solutions for common concerns, and research to support using cell phones in educational settings. Since I wrote that book, numerous teachers have started using students' cell phones in their instruction, both inside and outside the classroom. Their stories are unique but share some common threads. As I began communicating with these teachers, I realized how important it was to share their stories, beginning with how and why they decided to use students' cell phones, discussing any problems they encountered, and finishing with their reflections on the results they achieved.

In this book I present 16 teachers' cases about their experiences and activities with using cell phones: 11 from the United States and 5 from other countries. Of the 16, 10 teach language arts or social science courses and the other 6 teach math or science.

The purpose of this book is to illustrate many practical ways to use cell phones in learning: classroom groups, individual projects, homework outside of the classroom, field trips, and as communication tools for teachers, students, and parents. Every major subject area is represented in this book, as well as teachers from Grades 6–12. In addition, schools with students from a wide variety of social and economic strata are also represented, demonstrating that cell phones can be integrated in virtually any school district.

Each teacher in this book had a unique path to integrating cell phones into classroom learning. A few had problems, and many had to work around administrative policies. Some spent considerable time preparing lessons, whereas others were more spontaneous. Many had some wonderful unexpected outcomes. In the end, all of the teachers concluded that they would be using cell phones again in their future teaching.

General Overview of Case Studies

Following are some of the key questions that I am often asked by teachers, parents, and school administrators about using cell phones in learning. I have summarized the answers from the 16 teachers in this book to give broad perspectives on these questions.

Were there any discipline problems with students using cell phones inside of classroom learning? Most of the teachers in this book told me that they did not have any discipline problems when using the students' cell phones. Indeed, many of the teachers claimed that using the cell phones for learning actually cut down on discipline problems in school related to cell phone use. However, one teacher quickly dealt with a potential disciplinary issue by following through with consequences agreed upon before the class started using cell phones (the student had to donate money to a local charity), thus modeling consequences for actions. Many teachers mentioned that their discipline problems around cell phones decreased once they began setting up rules and cell phone safety guidelines and using the phones for learning, rather than spending class time taking them away and policing their use.

For example, in Case Study 4 you will read about Paul Wood, a teacher and technology coordinator in Texas, who found that cheating became a nonissue because the students were using their cell phones for learning out in the open, rather than hiding them in backpacks and under their desks. The students were mindful that they were being monitored and used the cell phones the right way.

Did using cell phones contribute to increased motivation or engagement in classroom instruction? Most teachers reported that motivation and engagement in the class activities increased when they were using the cell phones. For example, in Case Study 3, Katie Titler, a Spanish teacher in Wisconsin, found that many of her students went from being worried about or disengaged from oral language activities to being excited about oral language as a result of using their cell phones to record oral quizzes. Another example is Case Study 2, where Allison Riccardi, a Spanish teacher from Michigan, found that she "was amazed at how having [students] text sentences in Spanish really drew them not only into the activity, but also really helped them to understand the grammar behind what they were saying. In essence, using their cell phones in the classroom was what captured their attention."

Did the teachers intentionally start using cell phones in instruction?
Although most of the teachers in this book did begin with thoughtful
preparation and planning in using cell phones, a few teachers began using
student cell phones by accident. For example, in Case Study 15, Kipp Rogers,
a principal and math teacher in Virginia, started using cell phones because
he did not have enough calculators for all of his students to take a mandatory
standardized test, and realized that the students could use their cell phones to
calculate the problems.

**How did parents react to their children using their cell phones for
classroom learning?** Surprisingly enough, none of the teachers in this
book reported problems with parents being upset that their children were
using their cell phones for learning. As a matter of fact, some of the teachers
received thank-you notes from appreciative parents who were thrilled that
their children were learning how to use their cell phones appropriately and in
an educative way. Paul Wood said, "I received no negative comments and four
positive comments as well as some thank-yous."

How did the cell phones contribute to increased student learning?
In some cases, teachers mentioned that they were surprised how quickly
students became actively involved in the lesson planning process, rather than
just passively regurgitating information. These teachers found that once they
allowed their students to use cell phones in instruction, the students began
to suggest learning activities that they could do with their cell phones. In
Case Study 7, Judy Pederson, an English teacher in California, said, "At first,
being able to use their cell phones was instantly 'cool,' and grabbed students'
attention. After a while, it became a very convenient tool and students began
generating their own ideas for how to use the phones for projects." Therefore,
in some cases students began to take responsibility for their own learning and
their future learning by thinking of innovative ways to include their favorite
tool in the classroom lesson or activity.

What was the reaction of other teachers in their schools? Almost every
teacher in this book found there was a domino effect once they began to use
cell phones for learning in their classroom. In almost every case, there were no
other teachers at the school using student cell phones for learning when the
teacher began to use them. Yet, after the teachers completed the cell phone-
based project(s), they found a few other teachers in the school beginning to
use them as well. In addition, students also began to approach other teachers
and ask them if they could use their cell phones for learning activities. For

example, in Case Study 12, after Pennsylvania math teacher Jimbo Lamb did his first cell phone polling activity with his students, the word spread quickly through the school, and by the end of the same day, the journalism class was already interviewing Lamb, students, administrators, and other teachers about their views on cell phones in schools for the students' weekly news broadcast!

What about students who do not have a cell phone? How were they able to participate in these activities? There were a couple of teachers worried about doing cell phone–based activities when not every student owned a cell phone. However, they all found that, in the end, there were plenty of ways to manage the issue. Although only one of the teachers in this book had classrooms where 100% of the students had access to cell phones, every teacher found it fairly simple to work around the access issue. The most popular work-around was for teachers to group or pair up students so that there was one cell phone per group. In some cases, teachers simply selected a project where the students had an alternative to the cell phone. For example, Jimbo Lamb used a resource to record audio files at a toll-free number so that his math students could call in with their cell phones or a landline.

Did the students gain a new viewpoint on cell phones as a result of using them for learning? In many cases, the teachers claimed that their students had a "new perspective" on cell phones as a result of using them in learning. Many students began to see their cell phones as more than simply toys for entertainment; they began to view them as learning tools and lifelong data-gathering and disseminating devices.

How did the teachers deal with school policies that banned or restricted cell phones from campus? Each teacher's school district had differing policies governing cell phones. Some completely banned them, whereas others simply had restrictions on how and when they were allowed to be used during the school day. Yet, every teacher was able to find a way to work within the school policy to include cell phones in their teaching. Most teachers who wanted to use the cell phones during the school day were able to approach the administration and figure out an appropriate management system so that they could use the students' phones. For example, in Case Study 6, middle school reading teacher Tim Chase set up a management system approved by his administration so that when students were using their cell phones to take pictures for their class project during the school day, they wore "assignment badges."

While increased engagement and motivation is helpful, did using cell phones actually contribute to an increase in the level and quality of instruction? Although all of the teachers claimed an increase in motivation or engagement in the classroom curricula when cell phones were integrated into the lessons, in some cases the teachers were able to increase the level of instruction by using cell phones in place of more traditional methods. For example, Spanish teacher Katie Titler found that by using a web service that used cell phones to archive the audio recordings, she was able to more easily track her students' progress over time. She also found that cell phones allowed her homebound students to participate in oral speaking activities. Including homebound students and tracking oral language progress over time were activities that were very difficult to do with the more traditional methods of language labs and recording devices.

Did any teachers use cell phones for student management or communication? Some teachers found that using cell phone technology was a good way to better manage and increase communication with their students and parents. In Case Study 1, Larry Liu, an English teacher from Michigan, expanded his cell phone Facebook activity so that he was able to use Facebook to communicate homework help and answer questions from his students. He found that because most of his students were already actively using Facebook and their cell phones, it was easier to communicate with them via their favorite devices than by more traditional methods such as landlines or even email. Many of the teachers also set up office hours via cell phone (some via Twitter), where their students could text message or call them during designated evening hours.

Was it difficult to use student cell phones and couple them with Internet resources? Almost every teacher mentioned how surprisingly simple they found it to use student cell phones coupled with Internet resources in learning. Most teachers found that the most difficult part of integrating student cell phones was dealing with the policies that restricted cell phone use on the school campus.

General Highlights of the Book

The overview showed just some of the highlights from the 16 case studies you will read in Chapters 1 and 2. Each case study features how the teacher began using cell phones, school demographics, school policies, permission forms, rules and regulations developed, lesson plans, student and parent reactions, and problems that developed, as well as future lessons that the teachers have planned. Chapter 3 focuses on how teachers have used cell phones for administrative needs such as management and communication. Chapter 4 presents sample lesson plans using some of the resources mentioned in the 16 case studies in this book. Chapter 5 highlights some of the most successful steps for getting started using cell phones in learning. Included in Chapter 5 are current research findings and statistics to support the use of using student cell phones in classroom learning. Finally, Chapter 6 is a directory of free or low-cost Web 2.0 resources that couple with any basic cell phone.

Chapter 1

Case Studies from Language Arts and Social Sciences Classrooms

Case Study 1 ▪ **Larry Liu**

Northville High School, Northville, Michigan

Level	High School
Subject	Everyday Psychology (AP class)
Cell Phone Use	Outside the classroom
Cell Phone Activities	Text messaging, photo messaging, video messaging
Web 2.0 Resources	Facebook

The Inspiration

Larry Liu is a high school English and AP psychology teacher in Michigan. Since fall 2008, Liu has been using his students' cell phones to document everyday psychology happenings outside of the classroom to connect with classroom learning.

During the 2008–09 school year, Liu taught an elective course, AP Psychology, for eleventh and twelfth graders. One of his learning goals was for his students to be able to connect the concepts and ideas about psychology discussed in class with their everyday life experiences. When he spoke with his students about his learning goals, the students suggested using their cell phones to capture images and videos of their everyday life experiences and posting them on Facebook. Because almost all of his students were on Facebook daily, and they always had their cell phones with them, Liu was willing to try using both cell phones and Facebook. Liu did not begin his project with the intention of using student cell phones in learning, but found that by allowing students to use their cell phones, he was able to better meet his learning goals. Because both cell phones and Facebook are banned in Liu's high school, this activity was conducted only as a homework assignment.

School Demographics

Cell Phone Culture

The following describes the cell phone demographics in Liu's classes.

98% of the students had cell phones

Of the students who had cell phones:

92% could send and receive text messages
78% could send photos
62% could send video
75% had Bluetooth
47% had GPS

Social and Economic Data

2,229 students were enrolled in the school
85% of students pass the statewide reading proficiency
82% of students pass the statewide math proficiency
53% of adults in district have at least a bachelor's degree
95% of adults in district have at least a high school diploma

Economic Status
(from http://schoolmatters.com)

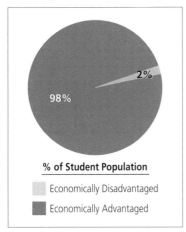

Enrollment by Race/Ethnicity
(from http://schoolmatters.com)

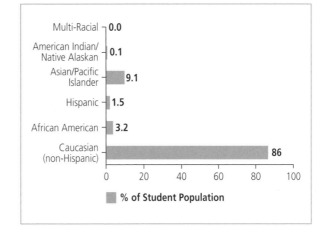

Project Example

Although Liu already had his own personal Facebook account, he decided to set up a separate account just for connecting with his students. This allowed him some privacy with his personal account, and an opportunity to talk with his students about appropriate Facebook postings, images, and profiles. Further, he cautioned the students that he was bound by law to report anything he saw on their Facebook pages that was illegal or inappropriate (such as drinking, drugs, or sexual images). He gave them fair warning (and repeated this warning often) that his students would be wise to clean up their profiles. He found that this activity by itself was a great opportunity for students to begin to develop positive digital footprints in their social networking sites and for them to take down anything that could be misconstrued or viewed as negative.

Once Liu had set up his new class profile, he became "friends" with each of his students. Then, the students were ready to begin the homework assignment. The students were asked to take pictures or videos with their cell phones when they encountered an everyday phenomenon that was linked to their class studies, and then send the media to their Facebook accounts with Liu's name as a tag. This allowed the media to post in both the students' accounts and Liu's class account. Because almost all of his students were on Facebook much of the time, they would often comment on the images. Then, before school each day, Liu would select a few pieces of the media from the class Facebook site to share in class. He would download the images and videos and put them on a flash drive so they could be viewed in class. Figure 1.1 shows the class Facebook page along with instructions for the psychology project.

School Policies

Cell phones are not permitted at Liu's school. Therefore, instead of trying to change policy, he took advantage of student cell phone use outside of the classroom.

Cell Phone Safety and Etiquette

To begin the project, Liu asked his students to clean up their Facebook profiles. He warned them often that he would report them if he viewed illegal or inappropriate images in their Facebook accounts. He took the time at the beginning of the project to educate his students on digital footprints and appropriate posting online.

Figure 1.1 Liu's class Facebook page with project instructions

Reactions

According to Liu, "Students have been rather receptive of the assignment. The first year it was debuted, students really jumped on board with it. Students get really excited about being able to share what they know because then they feel like they are a contributor to the class and on an equal level with me since they are teaching also. It's really great."

So far, Liu has found that parents' reactions have been favorable. Liu said, "Parents don't often comment on individual assignments, but the parents I've talked to at parent-teacher conferences have all been receptive of the idea of connecting school with life. Many are also quite pleased with the idea of teaching their kids how to responsibly use Facebook."

Hints and Tips from Larry Liu

- One of the most important pieces of this assignment actually didn't involve a tightrope walk of the school rules. Because the assignment was set as homework, the administrators were fully on board with the assignment from day one.

- The key for this assignment is communication. Because there is no set due date until the end of the semester, I have had to constantly remind my students about the assignment. Additionally, assignment quality becomes an issue. Fortunately, so far I've been able to pull out a few excellent examples early on and establish a very high bar for the rest of the classes to follow. This self-policed quality control is, in my opinion, one of the great strengths of social networking and is a valuable lesson for students to learn.

- Take every opportunity to talk about responsible Facebook usage. They say it takes repetition to learn things. When my students are thinking about posting pictures of their wild and crazy weekend party, I want them to hear my voice in the backs of their heads and make good decisions.

Unexpected Outcome

The project was such a great success for Liu that he has continued to use the Facebook account for class announcements, other class assignments, tutoring students, other school-related activities, and staying in touch with past students.

Future Plans

In the future, Liu would like to explore specific cell phone assignments that are still being taught in a more traditional manner.

See Chapter 4, Lesson Plan 11 for a tutorial on Mobile Facebook.

Case Study 2 ▪ **Allison Riccardi**

Gabriel Richard High School, Ann Arbor, Michigan

Level	Middle and High School (Grades 8–12)
Subject	Foreign Language (Spanish)
Cell Phone Use	Inside the classroom
Cell Phone Activities	Text messaging, audio recording with phone calls
Web 2.0 Resources	Wiffiti, Drop.io

The Inspiration

Allison Riccardi was a high school Spanish student teacher in a private Catholic school in Ann Arbor Michigan.

While Riccardi was student teaching, she was in a teacher education course that required her to pick an everyday technology tool and integrate the tool into her student teaching classroom instruction. With the permission of her cooperating teacher, Riccardi decided that she wanted to try using student cell phones. Originally, Riccardi thought she would do just a single required lesson with her students' cell phones, but after she saw how excited the students were during her initial project, she decided to incorporate more activities. Riccardi claims that most students find learning grammar in their Spanish courses to be dull and discovered that adding the cell phones helped to excite and engage her students in the grammar learning process.

School Demographics

Cell Phone Culture

The following describes the cell phone demographics in Riccardi's classes.

40–50%   of the students had cell phones

Of the students who had cell phones:

100%   could send text messages
100%   could take pictures with their cell phones

Social and Economic Data

Gabriel Richard High School is a private school.

464   students were enrolled in the school

Enrollment by Race/Ethnicity
(from www.edline.net/pages/Fr_Gabriel_Richard_HS)

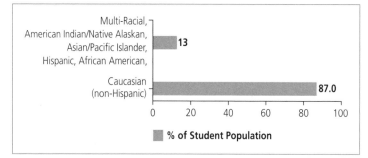

Project Example

During her student teaching, Riccardi completed two major cell phone projects in her Spanish class. One of Riccardi's learning goals was for her students to be able to correctly form the present subjunctive in Spanish. She wanted them to be able to distinguish between when they needed to use the subjunctive and when they needed to use the indicative tense. In addition, she wanted her students to correctly use the conjunctions that require subjunctive in spoken and written context.

After learning about a variety of web resources that couple with cell phones in her teacher education course, Riccardi concluded that proper use of conjunctions while text messaging would be an appropriate way to demonstrate their understanding.

To begin, Riccardi set up a free interactive web board at Wiffiti (www.wiffiti. com). Wiffiti allows anyone to create a blank screen online where students can send text messages. The messages immediately pop up on the board. Riccardi was especially pleased that at Wiffiti the text messages can be anonymous. She was hoping that anonymity would coax more participation from students who were usually shy about expressing themselves in class.

Next, Riccardi reviewed the Spanish conjunctions that require the subjunctive: those meaning "in order to," "unless," "without," "in case," "as long as," and "before." On the board, Riccardi wrote some Spanish *chatspeak*. (According to Wikipedia, chatspeak is a term for the abbreviations and slang used because of the necessary brevity of mobile phone text messaging—although its use is common on the Internet, including email and instant messaging. For example, changing the word text into "txt" would be considered chatspeak.) Students then tried to decipher meaning of each chatspeak message or term. For example, *ns qdms a ls 8 = nos quedamos a las ocho; para q = para que.*

After that, the students received a handout with these conjunctions and different possible subject pronouns that could come after these conjunctions. Students were asked to text a sentence using *para que* ("in order to") to her Wiffiti screen. They could use some of the chatspeak abbreviations if they chose. The Wiffiti screen was projected from Riccardi's computer to the whiteboard with an LCD projector. Students read their sentences on the Wiffiti screen, and the class corrected them out loud with Riccardi's assistance. Then, students wrote down any sentences that they liked or learned from on their sheet. Riccardi cleared the Wiffiti screen and moved on to the next conjunction, asking students to text a sentence that used it. She continued reviewing and making corrections. Figure 1.2 shows an image of the Wiffiti text messaging board with her student responses.

Figure 1.2 Example of Riccardi's Wiffiti text messaging board

Next came the oral portion of the activity. Riccardi set up a free account with Drop.io (a service that has been discontinued). Drop.io was a free Internet site that allowed people to call in and record audio files that were then posted on the site. Drop.io could be password protected or open to public view. Each account was given a voicemail number where students could call in and make audio recordings. After Riccardi gave her students the phone number to call, the students called in to Drop.io and recorded an exercise based on using conjunction and conjugating the subjunctive. Drop.io did not require students to have an account to call in and record.

Figure 1.3 is a copy of Riccardi's lesson plan from the Wiffiti and Drop.io Project.

Alternatives

Riccardi did not give an alternative to the assignment because she grouped students in pairs, making sure every pair had one cell phone with unlimited text messaging.

Figure 1.3 Sample lesson plan using Wiffiti and Drop.io

Lesson Plan: Wiffiti and Drop.io Project

Lesson objectives: Students will correctly form the present subjunctive. Students will correctly distinguish between when they need to use the subjunctive and when they need to use the indicative tenses. Students will correctly use the conjunctions that require subjunctive in spoken and written context.

Class period objective: Students will text a prompted sentence in Spanish with correct use of the subjunctive.

Technology benchmarks: Design and develop digital-age learning experiences and assessment (in this case a formative assessment). Facilitate and inspire student learning and creativity.

Materials: Computer with Internet access connected to projector, cell phones (one phone for every two students) with unlimited texting.

Stages of lesson: Review the Spanish conjunctions that require the subjunctive (in order to, unless, without, in case, as long as, before). On the board, write some Spanish chatspeak. Students try to decipher meaning (ns qdms a ls 8 = nos quedamos a las ocho, para q = para que). Students receive a handout with these conjunctions and different possible subject pronouns that could come after these conjunctions. This is where they will take notes.

Students text a sentence using *para que* ("in order to") to my Wiffiti screen. They can use some of the chatspeak abbreviations if they choose. Students read their sentences and class corrects them. Then students write down any sentences that they liked or learned from on their sheets.

I clear the Wiffiti screen, and we move to the next conjunction; students text a sentence with this. We continue reviewing and making corrections. Students practice using the conjunctions and conjugating the subjunctive orally by calling Drop.io and recording a book exercise.

Evaluation: This was more of a formative assessment, since it was an activity to check for understanding and progress. When students texted the sentences, the whole class had the opportunity to decide whether they were formed correctly or not. This enabled students to learn from their own mistakes and also to learn by looking critically at other sentences.

School Policies

Riccardi's school allows cell phones on campus, but students are not allowed to use them (seen or heard) during class sessions. Therefore, she decided to allow her students to take them out and use them (with her cooperating teachers' permission) during the class session and not focus on changing the school rules.

Cell Phone Safety and Etiquette

Riccardi did not discuss cell phone safety or etiquette with the students—they just jumped right in. Riccardi states, "I didn't go into rules. I simply described the activity and told students what they were supposed to be doing. Of course, it wouldn't hurt to be extremely precise about what they should not be doing."

Problems

Riccardi did not encounter any disruption of the learning process when using cell phones. However, she did have a few technical problems. For example: "There was one time when I tried this, and for some reason the comments were not posting to the Wiffiti board, which was quite frustrating. This did give students enough 'down time' to start getting off task and lose focus.

"Also, I had one group of students who posted sentences to the Wiffiti board that were in Spanish, but inappropriate (nothing vulgar, but still unrelated to the activity). In this case, I felt that the fact that they posted in Spanish was still better than them not getting involved at all, since they had demonstrated apathy towards learning Spanish all semester."

Reactions

Riccardi had an incredibly positive reaction from her students. "This was one of my best lessons with this particular class! I am always looking for new ways to get these students involved, because they love to create things, but they are not necessarily interested in learning the Spanish grammar that is part of our school's curriculum. They are also quite social and love to text and use technology. I was amazed at how having them text sentences in Spanish not only drew them into the activity, but also really helped them to understand the grammar behind what

Hints and Tips from Allison Riccardi

- Using cell phones is no different from any other technology—you must test the technology ahead of time!

- Make sure the text messaging sites are working properly and the phone calls are being recorded. For example, students could easily get frustrated if they did their oral language activity and Drop.io did not record them or if their text messages did not go through to Wiffiti.

they were saying. In essence, using their cell phones in the classroom was what captured their attention. I did have to stop a couple students a few times from texting something that was not related to the activity, but in my mind that was minor, since at least 95% of the students were engaged in texting for the assignment. I would rather have an overall focused class with a student or two texting unrelated messages now and then, than have a class silent and passive, pretending to pay attention during a traditional lesson."

Riccardi also found a lot of enthusiasm from her students when using the cell phones for the oral portion of the project, "The Drop.io activity was also a hit. Students do oral book activities all of the time, but this time, most of them were excited to do it, because they were leaving a message. Some of them even got creative with their messages and made side comments in Spanish. They were a lot of fun to listen to. Both of these activities were very successful for this class, and luckily my placement has the technology to support it. I would love to get more ideas of how to incorporate cell phones in learning, especially in the world languages classroom."

Riccardi also found that the vast majority of students were enthusiastic, even those students who did not normally show much excitement over the subject.

The Domino Effect

Although there were no teachers at this school using cell phones in class before Riccardi's project, she did inspire one other teacher in the school to begin thinking about using cell phones in learning activities. Her cooperating teacher showed some interest, but never created a lesson using cell phones. The administrators were surprised about the increase in use of this type of technology in her lessons and were interested in revising the school's cell phone policy. At one point before her project, the administrators were discussing whether or not to purchase a system that would block all cell phone signals throughout the school—to Riccardi's knowledge, this is no longer under consideration.

Future Plans

Riccardi definitely plans on using cell phones in her future teaching. "Yes! Probably more speaking activities using Drop.io. I would like to use cell phones as more of a catalyst for situational speaking exercises rather than just grammar drills. For example, one of my peers had students pretend that they stood up their date, and they had to leave a voicemail explaining what happened in the target language. These kinds of activities are inherently engaging, and using cell phones just spices them up that much more."

Case Study 3 ▪ **Katie Titler**

Pulaski High School, Pulaski, Wisconsin

Level	High School
Subject	Foreign Language (Spanish)
Cell Phone Use	Inside and outside the classroom
Cell Phone Activities	Audio recording with phone calls
Web 2.0 Resources	Voki

The Inspiration

Katie Titler is a high school Spanish teacher in Pulaski, Wisconsin. She started using student cell phones during the 2008–09 school year.

While networking on Twitter, Titler learned that some teachers were using students' cell phones for school learning experiences. She was intrigued, and as a result she began to brainstorm possibilities for using cell phones to enhance some of her own classroom learning goals. At the same time, she began to informally poll her students to get a sense of their feelings about using their own cell phones inside the classroom for learning. The students were overwhelmingly positive, and Titler learned that almost every student owned or had access to a cell phone. Once she knew of the access and enthusiasm, Titler kept this information to herself and waited for an opportune lesson where the cell phones would help to extend and enhance the learning experience. She began by using student cell phones to complete oral quizzes, and now is using them for a variety of learning activities.

School Demographics

Cell Phone Culture

The following describes the cell phone demographics in Titler's classes.

90–95%   of the students had cell phones

Of the students who had cell phones:

90–95%   could send and receive text messages
90–95%   could send and receive photos
70–80%   could send and receive videos

Social and Economic Data

1,200   students were enrolled in the school; varied greatly by socioeconomic level
84%   of students pass the statewide reading proficiency
87%   of students pass the statewide math proficiency
22%   of adults in district have at least a bachelor's degree
91%   of adults in district have at least a high school diploma

Economic Status
(from http://schoolmatters.com)

Enrollment by Race/Ethnicity
(from http://schoolmatters.com)

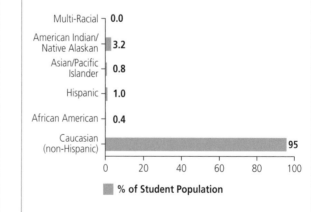

% of Student Population

☐ Economically Disadvantaged
■ Economically Advantaged

Project Example

As a language teacher, Titler often struggled with getting high school students to practice their oral language skills inside the classroom. Students tended to shy away from the oral language projects and exams. Titler discovered a free web resource called Voki (http://voki.com), which would allow her students to create their own avatars (similar to something they would do in a video game on a platform such as the Nintendo Wii) that would allow voice recordings via cell phones. Titler wondered if using Voki coupled with cell phones would increase her students enthusiasm and engagement in oral language activities. The other problem that Titler often faced with oral language exams was use of class time, which usually meant spending two or three 50-minute class sessions to test all of her students. (She would test them individually, away from the classroom.) Titler found it difficult to document the exam, relying on her memory and notes for grading. She realized that using Voki would allow her to cut down on the amount of class time she used for the oral language exams, and might increase students' enthusiasm for using their Spanish speaking skills.

To solve these concerns, Titler developed a cell phone project using Voki. The avatar created in Voki can have a unique look as well as audio. The audio can easily be created via a cell phone. Either Voki can call users when they are ready to record, or they can dial a 1-800 number to record the audio.

For the Voki speaking assessment, students were given a list of possible questions in the target language (Spanish) that integrated all the main concepts they had studied over the course of the semester. The students were then taken to the computer lab, where they were given the task to create their own personal avatar through the Voki site. Figure 1.4 is a picture of a Voki avatar created by one of Titler's Spanish III students.

Figure 1.4 Voki avatar

When it was time to add the voice to the avatar, Titler put the assessment questions into a box and asked each student to draw one question. Students then recorded their response to the question and saved their complete Voki avatar to the class account. Afterwards, Titler was able to go into the account and grade the assessments one by one. One useful aspect of this project was that if her students had questions about how they did on the assessment, Titler could go back and listen to it multiple times, and she could give them higher quality feedback.

Figure 1.5 shows the handout that Titler gave her Spanish II and III students.

Figure 1.5 Spanish lesson handout

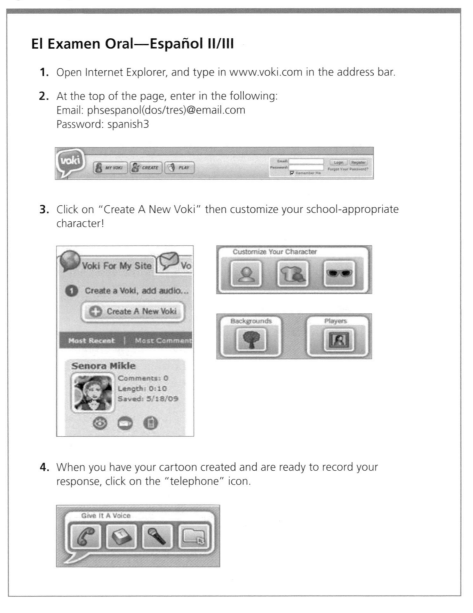

Figure 1.5, *Continued*

5. Then, once you receive your question, click on the link that reads (Or, Call The Old Fashioned Way). You will hear a greeting. At the beep, record your response.

6. Hit the # key when you are finished. Then, when prompted, hit 2 to save your message to your Voki character.

7. On your computer screen, you will see the box to the right, hit "Save." Name your audio with your Spanish first name and hour (Ej: Jorge 1, Tula2), then hit "Done." You are finished! Hit "Publish."

8. Give your scene the same name as the audio—Spanish first name and hour—and save. After the site processes your Voki avatar, hit "Close." You may listen to your avatar, and then hit "logout" to exit the site.

Alternatives

Although most of Titler's students did have access to a cell phone for the project, she provided alternatives for any student who did not have a cell phone (or who could not use their cell phone because they did not have enough calling minutes): She allowed students use her cell phone to record their Voki or, since the site has a 1-800 number, students could use a landline to call in their audio.

School Policies

Although cell phones are permitted in Titler's school, at the time there was no clause in the policy for instructional use. Therefore, with the assistance of the technology specialist and building administrators, Titler developed the special permission form for her project shown in Figure 1.6 on the following page.

Figure 1.6 Sample permission form

Permission Slip for Class-Related Cell Phone Use

With so much innovative technology available and utilized in the world today, I feel it is important to integrate what I can into my classes to help prepare students for their futures. During the course of the school year I will be implementing some newer methods of instruction and assessment, some of which will entail student use of cell phones for purposes such as recording speaking assessments, text message reminders of important class information (tests, quizzes, projects, etc.), and other classroom activities.

To apply this new technology, students will need to have access and authorization to use a cell phone. I am sending this permission slip to verify that your son/daughter has permission to use his/her cell phone for the sole classroom purposes explained above. If your son/daughter does not have access to a cell phone during the school day, I will have mine available for use, if permission is granted by you. I look forward to educating your son/daughter this year and implementing some exciting new strategies for instruction!

Sincerely,

Señora Titler

CELL PHONE USE AUTHORIZATION: **Activities and Assessments**
(Please read all options below, use a checkmark to indicate your preference and sign at the bottom.)

_____ Option 1: I give _____ permission to use his/her cell phone for Spanish classroom assessments and activities for the 2009–2010 school year.

_____ Option 2: I give _____ permission to use the teacher's phone for Spanish classroom assessments and activities for the 2009–2010 school year.

_____ Option 3: I *do not* give _____ permission to use his/her cell phone for Spanish classroom assessments and activities for the 2009–2010 school year.

Figure 1.6, *Continued*

I will not hold the Pulaski Community School district, the Spanish teacher or Pulaski High School liable for any phone charges incurred through the use of my child's cell phone for the specific classroom purposes stated above.

_____   _____

Parent/Guardian Signature   Date

CELL PHONE USE AUTHORIZATION:
Text Messages of Important Classroom Information
(Please read all options below, use a checkmark to indicate your preference(s) and sign at the bottom.)

_____ I give _____ permission to receive text messages to his/her cell phone about important class information such as reminders for tests, quizzes and other assignments for the 2009–2010 school year. His/her cell phone number is _____ .

_____ I, as the parent/guardian, would also like to receive text messages to my cell phone about important class information for my son/daughter such as reminders for tests, quizzes and other assignments for the 2009–2010 school year. My cell phone number is _____ .

_____ I do not wish for my son/daughter to receive any text messages about important class information.

I will not hold the Pulaski Community School district, the Spanish teacher or Pulaski High School liable for any phone charges incurred through the sending or receiving of text messages for the specific classroom purposes listed above. I also understand that a text message may not be sent for every important event, assessment or classroom activity.

_____   _____

Parent/Guardian Signature   Date

Cell Phone Safety and Etiquette

Although Titler did not present a formal lesson on cell phone safety or etiquette, she provided time for informal discussion with her students before, during, and after the project. She said the opportunity often arose as they were using cell phones to discuss appropriate and inappropriate uses of the devices in everyday life.

Reactions

Titler's students were very excited by the project. The students had not used cell phones for a classroom lesson before this project and were very open minded about being the first to try it out at their school. Many students commented on how "cool" it was to be able to actually create an avatar with their own voice speaking in Spanish. They enjoyed being able to listen to their own response as many times as they wanted. This immediate individual feedback was very useful for them. None of the parents had concerns about the project.

Problems

Although Titler did not have problems with her students using their cell phones inappropriately during the project, she did have a few small technical problems. First, she learned that students should use the 1-800 number to call in their audio recordings for Voki, rather than having Voki call their phones. (Voki seemed to be able to call only a few student phones at one time.) If students were all in the

---

Hints and Tips from Katie Titler

- Discuss ideas for cell phone projects with administrators, colleagues, and students to get feedback and guide you.

- Do a lot of research and exploration of the tools that you want to implement.

- Don't get frustrated if all does not go as exactly planned. You learn how to make improvements for next time by working through unforeseen problems.

---

computer lab to do the assignment, it could create a cell phone traffic jam! Second, Titler did have a small problem with an older computer lab that struggled with the Voki site. Her solution was to use a newer computer lab for the next class session, which also had better cell phone reception.

Unexpected Outcomes

Titler found that because Voki archived the audio recordings, she was able to easily track the students' progress over time. By having past records stored in Voki, she was able to go back (as well as have the students go back in time) and hear how much progress had been made. In addition, she liked that Voki allowed her home-bound students to participate in oral speaking activities.

The Domino Effect

Although no other teachers were using cell phones in learning at her school before Titler began her Voki project, this project did inspire a few other language teachers in her school to try the project with their students. Titler felt that once some teachers saw the positive results from the project, they began to think more seriously about using cell phones in their own learning.

Future Plans

Titler is definitely planning on doing the Voki project again. In addition, she is planning to use other features of her students' cell phones, specifically the text messaging. She is also researching using polling, interactive text message boards, and text alerts.

When asked if she has plans to use or expand her use of cell phones in the classroom into other areas or projects, Titler responded, "Yes, many! In fact, sometimes I can't sleep at night, because my brain is running rampant with new ideas I would like to try in the future."

Here are some of the main things she plans to implement in the upcoming school year, in addition to doing the Voki speaking assessment project again:

> **Voki.** In the beginning of the school year, to review a bit and have students get to know one another, she will have them write short bios

about themselves, including only their new Spanish names, that will later be recorded through a cell phone and added to their Voki avatar. They will then watch and listen to all the avatars as a class and try to guess who is who.

Gabcast/Phonecasting/Podcasts. She will continue to work on creating podcasts (which are also put on iTunes for easy student access) for both Spanish II and III classes. Her goal is to make one for the vocabulary and one for the grammar concepts for each unit/chapter. These are created through cell phone recordings.

Voicethread. She would like to create a "virtual language lesson." She is still exploring the possibilities, but wants to create a presentation/virtual lesson that students could see in class or access online to review or see if absent from class. Using a cell phone recording, she would overlay sound on a visual recorded presentation.

Text messages. She wants to send text message reminders to students and parents about important class information, such as quizzes, tests, project deadlines, and study tips. She has created a general permission slip that will go out with her syllabus in the fall, which gives both parents and students the option of receiving the class text message reminders.

Poll Everywhere/Wiffiti. (Something that works with the local cell phone carrier.) She is having trouble finding a site that will do what Poll Everywhere and Wiffiti can do but that will allow for text messages from the local cell phone carrier. She wants to have short, in-class discussions through text messaging to a live screen that can be viewed by the whole class.

See Chapter 4, Lesson Plan 4, for a tutorial on Voki.

Case Study 4 ▪ **Paul Wood**

Bishop Dunne Catholic School, Dallas, Texas

Level	High School
Subject	Religious Education
Cell Phone Use	Inside and outside the classroom
Cell Phone Activities	Text messaging
Web 2.0 Resources	Poll Everywhere, Twitter, and Google 411

The Inspiration

Paul Wood is a technology coordinator and a classroom teacher at Bishop Dunne Catholic School, a private Grade 6–12 school in Dallas, Texas. Besides his technology administrative duties, he teaches eleventh and twelfth graders in religious education.

Because of his background as a technology coordinator, Wood is always on the lookout for more bandwidth so that he can expand his students' digital learning opportunities in school. While observing the students at his school, Wood found that they were walking around with bandwidth available in their pockets that was woefully underused. Wood considered that he should show students what they could do with their phones other than texting and talking.

School Demographics

Cell Phone Culture

The following describes the cell phone demographics in Wood's classes.

70–80%   of the students had cell phones

Of the students who had cell phones:

100%   could send and receive text messages
100%   could take photos
70–80%   could take videos
50–60%   had GPS and/or Bluetooth
50–60%   had mobile Internet access

Social and Economic Data

Bishop Dunne Catholic School is a private school that draws from a wide variety of socioeconomic levels. Wood estimated that if the school were a public school, about 45 students (7.4%) would qualify for free or reduced lunch. The school gives away more than $1 million in scholarships to their students.

608   students were enrolled in the 6–12 school

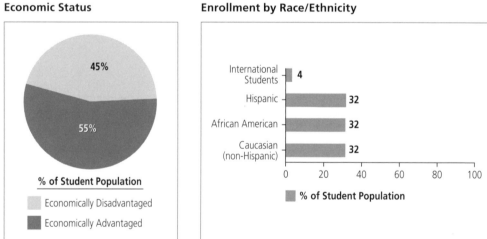

Economic Status

45%

55%

% of Student Population

☐ Economically Disadvantaged
■ Economically Advantaged

Enrollment by Race/Ethnicity

International Students — 4
Hispanic — 32
African American — 32
Caucasian (non-Hispanic) — 32

0   20   40   60   80   100

■ % of Student Population

Project Example

On a weekly basis in his Theology classroom, Wood coupled the use of web resources with cell phones. One of his first activities was with Poll Everywhere (www.polleverywhere.com). Poll Everywhere is a free web resource that allows anyone who can send a text message to participate in text messaging polls and brainstorming sessions. The text messages are instantaneously visible on an interactive online screen, which can be projected by an LCD projector in the classroom. Having his students participate in polls via their cell phones is how Wood begins his class on many days.

First he used Poll Everywhere to begin class by asking students to text message no more than three thought-provoking questions that would help to get the discussion started.

Next, Wood showed his students how to use Google 411 text messaging service, (www.google.com/mobile/sms/). Google 411 (now called Google SMS) allowed anyone to send a text message prompt to Google and receive an answer to the prompt. For example, you could send a text message to Google (466453) with the message "define astrology." You will then receive a text message back with the definition of astrology. Wood allowed his students to use Google 411 to look up words that they needed to define. According to Wood, "It got to the point where students would simply ask 'May we look it up on our phones?' and the answer was always 'yes' from me."

Finally, to connect and communicate more easily with his students, he set up a Twitter account and encouraged his students to text him via Twitter or directly to his cell phone if they had any questions or needed some extra help. Wood did put constraints and structures around the time he was available for text messaging, asking students to text between certain hours in the evenings.

Alternatives

Because Wood wanted to take advantage of the cell phones students already had, he also told the parents that they should not go out and buy their child a cell phone or change any current cell phone plans. He did not want parents to feel forced into spending money. He intentionally selected cell phone resources such as Google 411, Poll Everywhere, and Twitter, which all have alternative options for posting or sending information via the web or email. Thus, students without cell phones could still participate using computers at the school or at home.

School Policies

Although cell phones are permitted in Wood's school, the phones are not supposed to be seen or heard on campus during class sessions. Therefore, before using cell phones during class instruction, he spoke with the administrators in the school and received their approval to try using cell phones. Because Wood is also the technology coordinator, it was easier for him to work with the administration on adjusting the school policy. In doing so, he thought it was important to inform parents about the activities he was planning for the students' cell phones. Figure 1.7 shows the email message that Wood sent to the parents.

Figure 1.7 Sample informational email

Subject: **Sent to parents only**

Dear Parents:

I am very happy to be working with your children this year in theology. The class is a mixed class with juniors and seniors. You have already seen a couple of emails from me with information for your students. I will copy you on anything I send to them so that you know what is going on and should you ask the question "What are you doing in Theology?" and get the response I hear so many times, "Nothing," you will then have some information to work with.

I sent out a request for email addresses earlier, and I appreciate you parents responding. The survey is for the students to fill out, but if you wish to see it I will include you in the email to distribute the survey. As the Director of Technology and a permanent deacon for the Diocese of Dallas, I will try to use every resource I can think of to communicate with and educate your children. One of the things I would like to do is allow your children to text message me for help between certain hours. I am not looking for student phone numbers; I am merely trying to open an avenue of communication that the students use. Should I receive any text that I deem inappropriate, I will contact you. The only text from me to your child will be in response to a question or comment.

You may be thinking, "Well, my child does not have a cell phone." That is fine; do not go out and get one. If they do not have many texts available to them, do not change it for this class. In other words, do not spend money for any of this; there are many ways to make this communication happen. You need to do what you think is best for your child. I am still available by email or by appointment at the school.

Figure 1.7, *Continued*

Just so you have them somewhere, my school email is pwood@email.org; my home email is paulwood@email.net; my Google account, one that Google will make me use for forms, is prwood50@email.com. I would ask that you try to use the school email as the main way to contact me. My cell phone number so you will know who your child is texting if they do is 000-000-0000. I would ask that you not give that out and use it only in extreme emergency.

Due to my position, I also am asked to consult with schools on occasion as well as visit schools to try to learn from them and help Bishop Dunne to be the best school it can be; as a result I can already let you know that I will be gone for some classes during this semester. Due to the use of technology I will be in contact with your students and they will be turning in assignments to me electronically. I will require just about everything to be done electronically as opposed to using paper. Also, as a result of my vocation as a deacon, I will be attending a required retreat this fall. I will do everything possible to minimize any disruption to your student's schedule and education.

As always, if I can be of any help whatsoever, do not hesitate to contact me; you have almost every way possible of communicating with me in this email. Thank you for choosing Bishop Dunne and thank you for allowing me to participate in your student's education.

Paul Wood

Cell Phone Safety and Etiquette

Before Wood began using cell phones, he and his students agreed on a monetary fine for any cell phone use that was inappropriate. If the students used their cell phones in an unacceptable way during class, the student would pay the agreed fine, which would go to the local food pantry. Wood claims, "I only collected one time in two classes all semester."

Wood found that when the cell phones were used on a daily basis, the activities led to informal conversations about appropriate use and electronic communication protocol, as well as discussions about the different ways that students could use the tools available to them in their everyday lives as educative tools.

Hints and Tips from Paul Wood

- Start small and give it a try.

- Work with the students and model appropriate use with a cell phone.

- Make sure parents know about your learning goals before you start, and make sure the students understand that they do not have to have a cell phone. Have some alternatives ready in case some don't have unlimited text messaging or are unsure about using their phones.

- Have fun.

- Make sure you have a solid plan for consequences of inappropriate use. You must follow through!

- Make sure the administration understands what is going on. (In my case I made sure the dean of students knew what we were doing in case he came by class and students all had their phones out.)

Reactions

In general, the students were very positive and enjoyed the things they learned. The students also enjoyed trying to see who could answer the Poll Everywhere questions first. In addition, Wood believes that by using cell phones for learning, and having open discourse on the benefits of using cell phones productively as well as the concerns around cell phones, his students' perspective on their devices have changed over time.

Wood sent the email shown in Figure 1.7 to all the students and their parents or guardians before the class started. According to Wood, "I received no negative and four positive comments as well as some thank-you notes."

Problems

None! Wood felt that cheating became a non-issue because the students used their cell phones for learning out in the open, rather than hiding them in backpacks and under their desks. They were mindful that they were being monitored and were using the cell phones properly.

Unexpected Outcomes

Some of Wood's students came to him when they were doing presentations in his class and other classes to see if they could use his Poll Everywhere account as part of their presentations. "So I know that some other teachers saw the possibilities," he said.

The Domino Effect

Although Wood was the first at his school to implement cell phone activities, after they saw what he was doing, other teachers began using their students' cell phones. For example, one teacher engaged in podcasting with his social studies students.

Wood also found that some students were much quicker to jump in because the cell phone polling could be anonymous. When cell phones were used, he always achieved 100% poll responses from students!

Future Plans

Wood plans to continue using text messaging for questions, Poll Everywhere, and Google SMS for general class use. In addition, he is always looking for other ways to use the phones for actual class activities on a regular basis.

Case Study 5 ▪ **Rick Weinberg**

Pioneer Senior High School (Yorkshire-Pioneer Central School District), Yorkshire, New York

Level	High School
Subject	Foreign Language
Cell Phone Use	Inside and outside the classroom
Cell Phone Activities	Audio recording with phone calls
Web 2.0 Resources	Gcast

The Inspiration

Rick Weinberg is a technology development coordinator who works with more than 20 different school districts in New York. He had been considering using student cell phones to enhance his teaching for a long time, and in 2008 found an opportunity to use them with a French language teacher, Kathy Tevington.

Weinberg's inspiration to use student cell phones is part of his larger personal philosophy on teaching and learning. He believes strongly in differentiating instruction and is always looking for tools that will help create classroom opportunities to achieve this goal.

"I have always been into using technology that I think students would find interesting that can be used for learning," he says, "I felt that the cell phone was one of these devices. I saw educational author and blogger Will Richardson use his cell phone to answer the question 'What is the capital of Vermont?' I thought, since it is in your pocket and basically free, should we really be quizzing students on the capitals in fourth or fifth grade? I am a big proponent of using higher-order Bloom's Taxomony in the classroom. Cell phone technology may not always be higher order, yet I believe cell phones can be used in the classroom in the upper level of Bloom's. That is a primary goal of mine with using cell phones as a learning tool. I believe that students should be entrepreneurial and metacognitive with technology, and one of the best ways to do that using a cell phone is to get teachers to program applications for mobile devices. That is the catalyst for my thinking and what influenced me to use cell phones in the classroom."

School Demographics

Cell Phone Culture

The following describes the cell phone demographics in Weinberg's classes.

90–95% of the students had cell phones

Social and Economic Data

899 students were enrolled in the high school

87% of students pass the statewide reading proficiency

89% of students pass the statewide math proficiency

13% of adults in the district have at least a bachelor's degree

86% of adults in the district have at least a high school diploma

32% of students are classified as economically disadvantaged

Economic Status
(from http://schoolmatters.com)

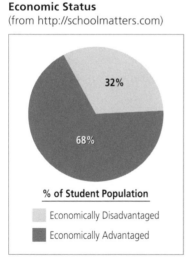

Enrollment by Race/Ethnicity
(from http://schoolmatters.com)

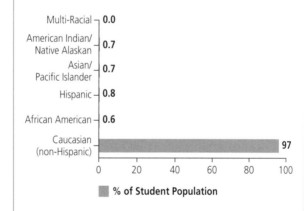

Project Example

In 2008, Weinberg conducted on-going professional development sessions with Kathy Tevington during her preparation period. "She asked me what I was learning that was new," Weinberg says, "I told her I was into cell phones for learning purposes, and she was interested. We talked about her curriculum and some things that she does in class, and we came up with podcasting using a verb tense that is rarely used in English, but often used in French." Next, Tevington created a rubric so that students knew what to expect and so that she knew how to grade the students. Tevington used a free resource, Gcast (no longer available; ipadio or Google Voice could be used instead) to create the podcasts. Each student created an account in Gcast and programmed the phone number into his or her cell phone. At the end of the project, Tevington gave all of her students a cell phone inquiry form (see Figure 1.8) to assess the students' understanding of their cell phones and the activities for the day.

Alternatives

An alternative was provided for those students who did not have their own cell phones in Tevington's class. Weinberg selected Gcast because it had a toll-free number; therefore, Tevington gave students without cell phones the option to use the classroom phone to record the podcast.

School Policies

Because the school's policy did not allow cell phones to be on during class instruction, Weinberg and Tevington made sure that the administrators in their school were aware of their project and asked the administrators for permission to use the student cell phones. Despite some apprehension, the administrators agreed to support the project. In addition, Tevington sent home a form before the activity to inform parents of the cell phone usage and to ask parents' permission for their children to use their cell phones for the learning activity.

Figure 1.8 Cell Phone Survey—Mrs. Tevington's French 4 Class

Cell Phone Survey

Please do not give your name.

1. Do you own a cell phone?

2. Do you have a texting plan?

3. Do you text during school?

4. Do you text during classes?

5. Do you ever text a fellow student about school work?

6. Because you were able to use your cell phone for class, were you off task and not focused on today's lesson?

7. During this class, French 4 on March 4th, did you call or text anyone or use your phone for any reason not specified for class today?

8. Would you like to see more lessons in Pioneer that involve using cell phone technology?

9. Do you feel that today's lesson involving a cell phone met Mrs. Tevington's lesson and curriculum objectives?

10. What about students who don't have a cell phone or can't afford phone calls or text messages for class work? Are these types of lessons fair for all students? Please explain your answer.

11. On a scale from 1 to 10, what was your excitement level (10 being most excited, 1 being not excited) concerning this lesson, knowing that you were going to be able to use your cell phone?

Cell Phone Safety and Etiquette

Before the project began, Weinberg talked with the class about appropriate use of cell phones during the project. In addition, Tevington handed out her final assessment survey at the end of the activity, which could also be used to discuss cell phone safety and use.

Hints and Tips from Rick Weinberg

- Make sure you "cross your T's and dot your I's." Plan, plan, plan before using student cell phones.

- Make sure the cell phone instructional use is transparent to administrators, parents, and students. One way to do this is by posting the lesson plans on the Internet. The lesson plans should include details of how the cell phones are to be used as instructional tools. Be specific about proposed activities with cell phones in permission forms sent home to parents.

- Help students understand that by learning how to use their cell phone as an instructional tool, they are creating a larger personal learning network (PLN) that will help them grow as professionals when they begin to enter the workforce. For example, if a student is interested in poetry, then the student should begin to network with professional writers and poets immediately (and not wait until they have finished high school or college). By utilizing cell phones and other digital resources, students can network with professionals from all around the world and begin to create professional collaborations before they finish high school.

Reactions

The students were excited and totally on task. They even showed off their podcasts to other students. Weinberg was not aware of any parent concerns over the project.

Problems

None! Not one student used a cell phone inappropriately during the project. Weinberg says that when he began to speak to the students about appropriate use of their cell phones, they told him that the talk was unnecessary and they knew they had to use their phones appropriately, and were excited to do so for the project.

Future Plans

Weinberg continues to promote the use of student tools and other digital devices that can aid in differentiating instruction. Recently, he demonstrated how to send mobile pictures, text, and videos to an online resource called Drop.io (since discontinued; Tumblr could be used instead) to a few teachers from the local middle school. He suggested that one way to use this mobile resource was to allow parents and students to text in their reactions to the student middle school science fair. The teachers were interested in proceeding in this direction for their science fair.

See Chapter 4, Lesson Plan 5, for a lesson plan on using ipadio (a recommended replacement for the discontinued Gcast) for creating oral language podcasts.

Case Study 6 ▪ **Tim Chase**

La Pine Middle School, La Pine, Oregon

Level	Middle School (Grades 5–8)
Subject	Reading
Cell Phone Use	Inside the classroom
Cell Phone Activities	Photography, uploading content to the Internet
Web 2.0 Resources	Drop.io, Poll Everywhere, Tumblr, YouTube, Gabcast or Gcast, Google 411

The Inspiration

Chase decided to use student cell phones because his school lacked the necessary equipment for his students to participate in a class project. He recalls, "I was frustrated that we didn't have a class set of cameras, but I needed the students to have some photos of themselves around the school. I began to tell them that they could bring a camera from home or use one of the ones we can check out from the media center, but then I realized that 70% of the people in class already were walking around with a camera that they couldn't use! That prompted a discussion with my administrators, and I was granted permission to use cell phones for instructional purposes in my classroom. Victory!"

School Demographics

Cell Phone Culture

The following describes the cell phone demographics in Chase's classes.

60–70%   of the students had cell phones

Of the students who had cell phones:

90–95%   could send text messages and photos
70–80%   could record and send video
10–20%   had GPS or Bluetooth capabilities
None   had mobile Internet on their cell phones

Social and Economic Data

520   students were enrolled in the middle school
72%   of students pass the statewide reading proficiency
62%   of students pass the statewide math proficiency
30%   of adults in the district have at least a bachelor's degree
93%   of adults in the district have at least a high school diploma

Economic Status
(from http://schoolmatters.com)

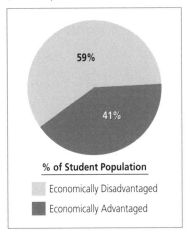

59%

41%

% of Student Population

 Economically Disadvantaged

Economically Advantaged

Enrollment by Race/Ethnicity
(from http://schoolmatters.com)

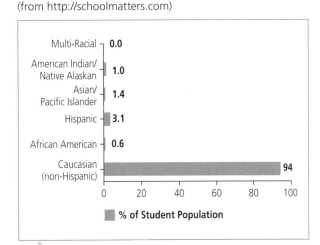

Multi-Racial **0.0**
American Indian/ Native Alaskan **1.0**
Asian/ Pacific Islander **1.4**
Hispanic **3.1**
African American **0.6**
Caucasian (non-Hispanic) **94**

0   20   40   60   80   100

% of Student Population

Project Example

Chase explains how he came to use cell phones in his classroom: "Students were demonstrating skill with standard Microsoft Office applications, and they needed pictures of their school day to complete the project. They took pictures of themselves, used BigHugeLabs (http://bighugelabs.com) to make a fancy badge to wear while they were out 'on assignment,' and then used their phones to take the action shots they needed for the project."

Figure 1.9 is a copy of the handout from the project.

Figure 1.9 Project handout

Cell Phones in Action!

(Only put your cell phone into action if you know for sure that sending text/pics/vids will not cost your family money. Please call home and ask if you don't know.)

Register Your Phone

First, please send a text message with YOUR NAME to tim.chase@email.com. Do this whether you'll be using phones to send pics to the website or not—it's my way of collecting phone numbers for the group.

Send a Pic to Tumblr

You can add photos to our Ashland 2009 Website. Try it before we go … take a photo or a video and send it to 333@tumblr.com (you may want to temporarily add the contact to your phone).

Leave a Voice Message on our Trip Website

000-000-0000 x 5364

Pics and Vids at: ashland.tumblr.com

MP3 voice messages at: Drop.io/ashland

Alternatives

Chase did not have an alternative to using cell phones in this project because the students worked in groups, and he made sure there was at least one student cell phone available in each group of students.

School Policies

The school policy where Chase teaches stated that cell phones were allowed on campus and could be used during class only for instructional purposes. When Chase approached the administrators, he found that they were supportive but apprehensive. Ultimately they gave their approval for the project.

Chase went an extra step to let the other teachers in the school know that his students were allowed to use their cell phones during the school day for his project. Chase explains, "Mostly I knew they'd get in deep doodoo if another teacher saw them with cell phones out during the school day, so for their photo project (using the phones), they had to wear their 'on assignment' badges."

Cell Phone Safety and Etiquette

Chase did discuss cell phone safety with his students before, during, and after the project.

Reactions

"Kids like using their phones in school. The phones weren't any better than traditional cameras, and the quality was much worse than if they'd borrowed the school cameras, but we don't have the resources to supply every kid with a camera—we don't have a class set of cameras to check out. So this was a good way around that problem."

Problems

Tim did not encounter any problems with the students using their cell phones for this project.

The Domino Effect

There were no others teachers at Chase's middle school using student cell phones for learning before Chase used them. He was able to inspire one other teacher to try using student cell phones.

Future Plans

Chase states: "My job assignment is changing to a student population with potentially very few cell phones, so I have no immediate plans.

"When I take a student group to the Oregon Shakespeare Festival in Ashland in the spring, I'll use their cell phones to communicate with the students from my laptop, and I may try again to have them get photos into a central place online."

Case Study 7 ▪ **Judy Pederson**

Valley High School, Santa Ana, California

Level	High School (Grade 9)
Subject	Language arts
Cell Phone Use	Inside and outside the classroom
Cell Phone Activities	Text messaging, phone calls
Web 2.0 Resources	ChaCha, Poll Everywhere, Twitter, Blogger Mobile, Textnovel, Flickr Mobile

The Inspiration

Judy Pederson is a ninth grade English teacher in Santa Ana, California. Most of her students are first-generation Americans whose primary home language is Spanish.

Pederson was working on her master's degree in education technology when she noticed that most of her students had their own cell phones. Working in a school where very few of her students had Internet or even computer access outside of school, Pederson realized that student cell phones might be one way to connect her students to learning via Internet sites outside and inside of school. She searched the Internet and bookstores for ideas on how to use student cell phones in learning and came across the blog Cellphonesinlearning.com (the author's blog). She found that the blog provided many ready-to-use suggestions on how to couple basic phones with learning and decided to try a few activities. She began by using cell phones for polling students.

School Demographics

Cell Phone Culture

The following describes the cell phone demographics in Pederson's classes.

60–70%   of the students had cell phones

Of the students who had cell phones:

80–90%   could send text messages
90–95%   could take and send photos
30–40%   had mobile Internet

Social and Economic Data

3,067   students were enrolled in middle and high school
54%   of students pass the statewide reading proficiency
59%   of students pass the statewide math proficiency
16%   of adults in the district have at least a bachelor's degree
53%   of adults in the district have at least a high school diploma

Economic Status
(from http://schoolmatters.com)

Enrollment by Race/Ethnicity
(from http://schoolmatters.com)

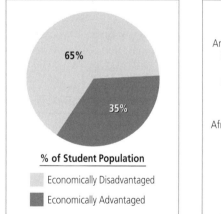

65%

35%

% of Student Population

▢ Economically Disadvantaged
■ Economically Advantaged

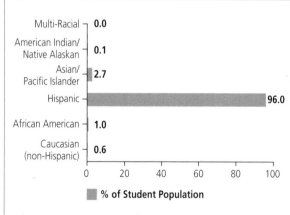

Multi-Racial	0.0
American Indian/Native Alaskan	0.1
Asian/Pacific Islander	2.7
Hispanic	96.0
African American	1.0
Caucasian (non-Hispanic)	0.6

0   20   40   60   80   100

■ **% of Student Population**

Project Examples

Pederson's first project used Poll Everywhere to check for students' comprehension during a lesson, or as a pre-quiz. Students also sent her questions and answers that they wanted her to use the next day. Next, Pederson set up student blogs with Blogger (www. blogger.com). She showed her students how to submit data to blog posts via their cell phones. Students then added pictures, videos, or even text message posts. One project required students to interview their parents. Several students used the video recorders on their cell phones to capture the interviews.

After the success with blogging, Pederson introduced her students to Twitter. Using Twitter, her students subscribed to a line-by-line Twitter production of Romeo and Juliet. The lines of the play were sent out every 15 minutes, and the play lasted a couple of months. Every day, those who were following the play would discuss which part of the play was being broadcast. It was a great way to isolate each line.

Beyond whole-class Twitter projects, some students elected to use Twitter in other creative ways. For example, one student published a line-by-line diary for a family member who was the subject of a research project. In addition to literary projects, Pederson has encouraged her students to use Twitter to gather information on other schools by engaging with educators around the globe. Besides classroom projects, Pederson also sent homework and study reminders using Twitter.

Pederson also allowed her students to use ChaCha (a free text messaging service where one can ask a question, and the answer will be sent to the student's cell phone; http://chacha.com). During collaborative group work, students were allowed to use ChaCha to gather additional information. The students had to write their own questions based on the lesson.

Pederson's students could also use text messaging to contact her outside of school. Students could text (or call) her any time until 9:00 p.m. to ask for clarification on an assignment.

Alternatives

Not all of Pederson's students owned a cell phone. Therefore, she often relied on groups or non–cell-phone options for assignments.

School Policies

Cell phones were allowed on campus and could be used during class only for instructional purposes. When Pederson began, her administrators did not know about the project. They are now supporting her use of student cell phones in her teaching.

Cell Phone Safety and Etiquette

Pederson did speak with her students about cell phone safety and etiquette before, during, and after the project. Pederson emphasized issues such as the public nature of text messaging and how students need to be mindful of every message they send. She developed rules that she expected her students to stick with: Phones need to be off and out of sight unless I explicitly state the phones can be in use. Phones are to be used for intended purposes only. Misuse of a phone during class would result in confiscation and possible banning of the phone in the future. Pederson believes the benefits of using cell phones outweigh the occurences of one or two off-topic text messages (such as a quick text to a friend). In general, she found that her students were respectful with their cell phone use and did not abuse the privilege. She did not have to confiscate any cell phones.

Reactions

At first, being able to use their cell phones was instantly "cool" and grabbed students' attention. After a while, cell phones became a very convenient tool, and students began generating their own ideas for how to use the phones for projects. Pederson has not heard from any parents concerning the use of cell phones.

Problems

Pederson had a few technical issues with cell phone plans in California (one phone plan in particular would not work with a few of the resources). She also found that students took time to catch on to how Twitter works and needed a lot of guidance to understand the purpose and learning potential of the environment.

Hints and Tips from Judy Pederson

- Start with one project.

- Do something that most students can do on their phones—perhaps start with text messaging.

- Include students in the planning—they know what their phones can do. Most students have cameras in their phones; that would be a good place to start, too.

Future Plans

Pederson definitely plans on using cell phones in her future teaching. "Absolutely. I have a new principal who is very supportive of 21st-century learning. When the faculty wanted to ban cell phones, I went in to tell her about my projects. On her desk was a copy of *Toys to Tools: Connecting Student Cell Phones to Education* (author Liz Kolb's first ISTE book). Happily, we will not be banning cell phones. As more students have cell phones and as more cell phones have better and better apps, I intend to use this mini-computer more often."

See Chapter 4, Lesson Plan 7, for a lesson plan on using ChaCha.

Case Study 8 ▪ **Carla Dolman**

Craik High School, Craik, Saskatchewan, Canada

Level	Grades 8–9
Subject	English Language Arts
Cell Phone Use	Inside the classroom
Cell Phone Activities	Taking photos
Web 2.0 Resources	None

The Inspiration

Carla Dolman is an eighth and ninth grade English and literacy teacher in Saskatchewan Canada at Craik High School. Dolman has been using her students' cell phones in learning since 2007.

According to Dolman, her inspiration for using her students' cell phones came from "the fact that they were perceived as a problem. My principal and I decided to see if we could turn the negative into a positive." The technology coordinator in the school district, Dean Shareski, worked with Dolman on turning the students' cell phones into a classroom learning tool. They began by developing some goals for learning, which included using cell phones for learning, appropriate use of cell phones ethically and legally, using cell phones for scheduling and organization, using text messages to discuss literature with literature circles, engaging disengaged learners, and tracking assignments, projects, and general academic progress. They decided to begin with Dolman's eighth and ninth grade English language arts students and asked them to bring in their cell phones to class one day in January 2008. If students did not have a cell phone, they could use an Internet resource, mysask.com, for text messaging.

School Demographics

Cell Phone Culture

The following describes the cell phone demographics in Dolman's classes.

40%   of the students had cell phones

Of the students who had cell phones:

100%   could send and receive text messages
100%   could take photos and videos via their cell phones
100%   could use Bluetooth
100%   could use the Internet

Project Example

Although only about 40% of students had their own cell phones, the students with cell phones were willing to share. Dolman began by using the text messaging and the alarm features of students' phones. These features were useful in reminding students about homework assignments and upcoming exams. As she became more savvy and learned what functions the students had on their phones, she began to expand the features they used, such as Bluetooth features for easy information sharing, video, and audio recording. One of the best projects for student cell phones was literature circles. For the literature circles, Dolman divided her students into smaller groups to discuss different aspects of a particular book. In the past, she had found it difficult to monitor the activities taking place in each group. However, by integrating one student cell phone per group, she had students use the video functions on their phones to record the group discussions and then send them to Dolman's phone. This allowed Dolman to watch and listen to each group discussion without missing a second.

Alternatives

Dolman did not have alternative lessons because she put the students into groups, eliminating the need to worry about each student having a cell phone. Each group had at least one cell phone.

School Policies

Cell phones are allowed on campus and can be used during class only for instructional purposes.

Cell Phone Safety and Etiquette

Dolman and her students developed the classroom rules and regulations for cell phone use together. They discussed appropriate use and appropriate consequences for breaking the rules. She posted the guidelines on the wall and often had discussions of etiquette, manners, privacy, and safety when using the cell phones. This gave students a sense of responsibility and ownership over the privilege of being able to use their cell phones for in-class learning.

Reactions

Dolman said her students were excited, shocked, energetic, positive, and focused, and they couldn't believe that adults were going to trust them to use their cell phones.

No students violated the rules set up for cell phone use. Dolman believes that students were too busy learning with their phones to worry about abusing the privilege! Dolman enjoyed learning about student cell phone culture and embraced the new knowledge by using it in her assignments (such as the Bluetooth function that her students taught her). Although students were divided on whether they found that cell phones enhanced their learning, there was consensus that cell phones helped with motivation because they made the assignments more fun! The students were well aware of the difference between text message "lingo" and proper English grammar.

Initially some parents were skeptical, but they soon began to change their viewpoints as they witnessed the learning activities with cell phones. Dolman did not hear from parents during the activities, but after the projects a few told her that they were very supportive and positive about what had taken place.

Problems

Dolman did not encounter any problems; in fact, she found that class disruptions due to cell phones decreased dramatically. She believed that by giving students guidelines around cell phone use and teaching them about appropriate use, she avoided major problems.

Hints and Tips from Carla Dolman

Dolman suggests that teachers "Start slow—don't be scared that the students will know more about the phone than you will."

Unexpected Outcomes

Dolman found that her students learned a lot about the capabilities of their cell phones and how to use them to accomplish academic tasks inside and outside of school.

The Domino Effect

Dolman did influence one other teacher in the school to try using cell phones in the classroom.

Future Plans

Dolman plans on focusing more on the image and video-capture capabilities of her students' cell phones.

Case Study 9 ▪ **Stephen Collis**

Northern Beaches Christian School, Sydney, Australia

Level	High School (Grades 8–12)
Subject	Geography and English
Cell Phone Use	Inside and outside the classroom
Cell Phone Activities	Audio blogging
Web 2.0 Resources	Utterli (formerly Utterz)

The Inspiration

Stephen Collis is the Head of Innovation at Northern Beaches Christian School (NBCS), an independent K–12 school in Sydney, Australia.

Collis explains that his inspiration came from learning about a specific function of the mobile phone. According to Collis, "When I heard about the possibility of audio blogging by ringing a local telephone number, I realized this would bypass the myriad of issues that arise when you try to use audio with computers. Audio with computers is confined to the computer itself, which is not very portable, and there are always problems with headsets and soundcards. However, everyone has a telephone, and everyone knows how to use one."

School Demographics

Cell Phone Culture

The following describes the cell phone demographics in Collis' classes.

100%   of the students had cell phones

Of the students with cell phones:

100%   could send text messages
70–80%   could send photos
40–50%   could take and send videos
10–20%   had access to GPS or Bluetooth

Social and Economic Data

1,200   students were enrolled in the school

Project Example

Collis gives two examples of teachers he works with in Australia who have used student cell phones in their classrooms. First, he worked with geography teacher Cherie Low, whose ninth grade students used their cell phones to capture pictures of Australian flora and fauna. The students used a free online resource called Utterli, which allowed them to send pictures directly from their phones to their project website (http://australianenvironment.wordpress.com; Figure 1.10).

Figure 1.10 Geography project website

Next Collis worked with Su Temlett. Temlett had her twelfth grade English students use their cell phones to post audio responses on their class blog (Figure 1.11). The students were asked to read the poetry of William Wordsworth in a natural setting outside of school, and then record a reflection in that setting via their cell phone. The goal was to help them understand the root of nature in the poetry by being in a natural setting (http://wordsworthreflections.wordpress.com).

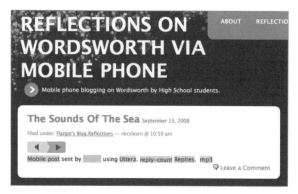

Figure 1.11 Temlett's English class blog

Alternatives

Because there were some students who could not use their cell phones, both of the teachers provided an alternative to using cell phones in the assignment. The students were able to use a landline for the audio recordings and a regular camera (in this case the students could upload images manually) for the photo project.

School Policies

For both teachers and students, cell phones were allowed on campus and allowed to be used in class for instructional purposes. As an extra precaution and important piece of parent communication, Temlett sent a letter home to inform parents of the English poetry project (see Figure 1.12).

Figure 1.12 Sample permission form

20 June 2008

Dear Parent/Guardian,

I am writing to let you know about an exciting project involving your son/daughter.

The project will be run with Year 11 Advanced English in collaboration with English teacher (and English Learning Area Manager) Mrs. Su Temlett.

The project is entitled 'Mobile Poetry Blogging' and will involve students posting a blog (a blog is simply a journal entry done on computer) once a week related to their studies of poetry by William Wordsworth. Student blogs will appear online and will be accessible freely over the Internet.

Students will be challenged to make their blogs of such quality that the final blog website, where all the blogs will be found, might gain a good reputation amongst other teachers and students around the world who may also be studying Wordsworth in the future.

This project should be highly beneficial to the students' learning, since their class work will be feeding into a larger, public, arena.

Although the students will be able to create their blogs from any computer connected to the Internet, they will also be able to publish directly from a mobile phone. This creates some unique possibilities. With a mobile phone, students will be able to record audio directly to the Internet, by dialing a number and speaking, and take images or videos and send them directly to their online blog using email. Now, Wordsworth's poetry is concerned with truth and beauty in nature, and he perceives human industry and city living to have an alienation effect on our connection with nature. Students will be able to post blogs about nature, while sitting in a valley or on the beach, or on a busy polluted road. This a way for them to take their learning process on the road, so to speak, which ought to make their understanding less artificial than if relying solely on discussion inside a classroom.

Three issues need to be considered and managed in regards to this project.

Issue #1: The students' privacy is at stake, since the Internet is open to anyone in the world.

Management: Students will be entirely anonymous and will be strictly instructed not to post personally identifiable information, or images or videos of themselves. Students' first names will not be used. Students will be very carefully trained over what they can and can't post. Mrs Temlett and myself will be able to monitor the blogs to enforce this, and if necessary, delete blogs.

Continued

Figure 1.12, *Continued*

Issue #2: Copyright on material created by students cannot be enforced, since online material can easily be copied and copyright undermined, especially when the material is posted to the Internet anonymously, as is the case in this project. The service we will use to publish from the mobile phones is www.utterz.com. You can read their terms and conditions here: www.utterz.com/terms.php.

Of particular interest is this: "You own all content that you post on Utterz, and by posting any content, you grant Utterz the perpetual, irrevocable, non-exclusive, sublicensable right to display that content in any form on any Utterz Service (whether by phone or over the Internet) or anywhere else, without limitation. You also agree that you will only use any Content you view at Utterz for your own personal, non-commercial use."

In other words, Utterz reserves the right to republish the blogs in multiple forms.

Management: In this project, students will not be publishing any material that is likely to be of any commercial worth! Nevertheless, students and parents need to give permission to participate in the project, knowing that, practically speaking, when material is posted freely to the Internet, the author's copyright (the student's copyright) is unlikely to be enforceable, and it is possible the blogs could be reproduced. A good rule of thumb with the Internet in general is, "If you publish it online, you immediately relinquish control of it."

I'll make a final comment that if the blogs are reproduced and republished at other websites, it will be a great compliment to the quality of the students' work. If, for instance, some of their text shows up in Wikipedia, I would not, for one, be distressed. However, being anonymous, students could not claim public credit.

Issue #3: The project will require students have access to certain technologies.

Management: Students will need at least access to a computer with an Internet connection, and ideally have regular access to a mobile phone, even if this is not their mobile phone. They will need to bring this phone into school for one nominated to be set up. If students record audio from their mobile phone, they'll be charged for a local landline call. They could blog from their home phone for the cost of a local call instead, but this defeats the purpose.

Students will be posting one or two blogs a week for about 6 weeks. So, their mobile phone costs could add up to the cost of 12 local calls over the duration of the project, which does not seem to me to be excessive.

To send images and video directly "on the spot" from their mobiles they'll need to have email access from their mobile phone. Now, I suspect many students will not have this feature, but there is an easy alternative: students can send images

Figure 1.12, *Continued*

---

or video from home by transferring them from their mobile phone to their home computer.

Note that this project is experimental. It is the first project of its kind to be run at the school, and will undoubtedly be a learning experience for all. As such, I am particularly keen to hear any comments or concerns you have.

The students will be excited to know that the project will be showcased at the Expanding Learning Horizons conference in Victoria in August, and probably at a range of other venues over the following months. Using mobile phones for learning is talked about a lot, but there are not many schools actually acting on the ideas, so there will be interest in what we achieve at NBCS.

Cell Phone Safety and Etiquette

Both teachers discussed mobile safety and etiquette before they began their projects (much of this was included in the letter home to parents before the beginning of the project).

Reactions

Collis found that both parents and students had very positive reactions to both projects: "Overwhelmingly strong. The great motivator was that people were coming to the website and actually listening to them. They saw the web counter and map show this, and they had a lot of comments on their blogs."

As for administrator reaction, Collis is the administration and was the one who initiated the idea of using student cell phones coupled with Utterli: "Well, I am the administration, so, very supportive! I advertised the idea to staff, and Temlett and Low responded."

Problems

Collis reports: "No complaints. I asked students about their parent's reactions and they were very positive. One student said 'my mom said she wished she had done this when she was in school.'"

"My principal appointed me as the Senior Executive of the school in order that this sort of project could run without obstacle. I can invite staff to try new ideas and then approve the projects myself.

"The biggest success was the Wordsworth project. I think the greatest power in cell phones lies with the audio capture when used together with Web 2.0 phone blogging services, coupled with the potentially worldwide audience."

Hints and Tips from Stephen Collis

The project was slightly fiddly to get going, because every student needed to be registered with www.utterli.com, and then their Utterli account had to be linked to the Wordpress website that the final recordings were published to (http://wordsworthreflections.wordpress.com). It ended up working fine, but it took a couple of hours to set them all up.

Unexpected Outcomes

According to Collis, "The main outcome was student engagement and enthusiasm, which we had hoped for, but this was unexpectedly strong. The students took the reflection tasks very seriously indeed. You can hear their sincerity in the broadcasts at the website."

The Domino Effect

"The project had a huge domino effect in the general area of online student publishing," says Collis." The project confirmed for me the value of online publishing, because students take on an entirely new perspective on their studies. Since 2008 we've replicated the principle of student publishing across the whole school, and it is now almost standard practice for our teachers to set up a website for their class and have students publish the best of what they are doing. We've linked all these projects to one central portal, www.realaudienceproject.com. You can see resources for online student publishing at http://realaudienceproject.wikispaces.com."

Future Plans

Collis reports, "Utterli announced that they were canceling their Australian dial-in numbers, so we have been unable to reproduce the project." The service has since been discontinued completely. According to Collis, "There are similar services such as ipadio (www.ipadio.com) that would allow the project to be reproduced."

Case Study 10 ▪ **Toni Twiss**

Schools in Hamilton, New Zealand

Level	Primary (Grade 8)
	Secondary (Grades 9 and 12)
Subject	Social Sciences
Cell Phone Use	Inside the classroom
Cell Phone Activities	Taking photos, text messaging
Web 2.0 Resources	Poll Everywhere, Utterli, YouTube, Qipit, Opera Mini, downloading applications (e.g., graphics calculator)

The Inspiration

Toni Twiss is an eLearning and Curriculum Advisor to Secondary Schools. She began a research study on using mobile phones in classroom learning in New Zealand in 2008. The phones were donated by Vodafone New Zealand, and her study was made possible by the New Zealand Ministry of Education. Her major focus was accessing the Internet rather than using specific applications, because many of these are not available in New Zealand. She worked with three different grade levels and a few different teachers on using student cell phones in learning.

According to Twiss, "My classroom configuration consisted of 15 G5 Macs on benches around the classroom and an interactive whiteboard. Access to these resources completely changed my teaching philosophy and methods. Through the technology available to me, I truly had the opportunity to become a facilitator of information, rather than be in the position of holding all the knowledge, which I drip-fed to students. I began to create tasks for students that allowed them to tap into the vast amounts of information available online. Students began to develop valuable information-gathering skills. My role became one that motivated students to find information and gave them ideas as to how to process this information.

"Over time, my classroom teaching style began to focus more and more on how to get students critically analyzing the information they were finding. Learning was becoming personalized as students had the ability to follow the angles that they enjoyed within the set of guidelines given. Learning became collaborative as students were encouraged to share their findings with others in the class through oral presentation and question-and-answer sessions—initially modeled by me as the teacher, but in time adopted by the students as they took ownership of their own learning and were empowered to lead class discussions.

"I realized that the type of learning that my students were experiencing in my classroom was not possible to recreate in a 'computer lab' environment. The technology was too obtrusive and became the focus of the lesson, rather than the content. The type of technology that was available to me in my classroom is not financially practical in every classroom. However, many of our students are bringing their cell phones to school every day, most of which are capable of recreating the teaching style I was employing in my classroom. What's more, the students enjoy using their phones."

School Demographics

Cell Phone Culture

The following describes the cell phone demographics in Twiss' classes.

90–95%   of the students had cell phones

Of the students who had cell phones:

100%	could take and send photos
90–95%	could send and receive text messages
80–90%	could take and send videos
70–80%	had GPS and/or Bluetooth
70–80%	had mobile Internet

Project Example

Twiss developed a research project with three different classes of students, two secondary and one primary. Her goal was to explore the potential for using a class set of Internet-ready mobile phones with no associated charges for calls or data. They used a variety of tools already installed on the phones such as video and voice recorders. However, the greatest focus was on using the phones to access the

Internet throughout class, either as part of a teacher-led activity or in response to students' own needs.

Teachers used a hybrid of highly planned mobile phone activities, as well as some impromptu activities. After the teachers were shown a number of different tools and resources that they could use on the mobile phones, they each selected the tool or tools that they thought would work best for their learners. All of the teachers created polls for their students using Poll Everywhere. In addition, they all used the audio and video recording features of the phones for class projects.

A free application called Opera Mini was installed on all the students' phones so that they could easily search the Internet. This gave students great clarity of the text on the screen, the ability to customize, the ability to view any website (mobile-ready or not), and the ability to sync the homepage with class bookmarks.

All three teachers had their students participate in mobile phone polling using Poll Everywhere (www.polleverywhere.com).

The Eighth Graders

The eighth grade students had access to their mobile phones all day, in all classes. The focus of their project was the upcoming 2008 election in New Zealand. The students could use their phones to answer questions they had about the election. For example, they used their mobile phones to find out which electorate they belonged to, and which electorate read newspapers about current election news. The eighth grade students also used the free texting poll on Poll Everywhere (where they could submit text messages to a blank screen) to consider all the different ways that money is spent in New Zealand.

In addition, the students used mobile phones to complete a dance project for school. Each student was in charge of a different piece of the "evolution of dance." They used YouTube for dance tutorials, and put videos on their mobile phones related to the portion of the dance they were to learn. This allowed the students to always have the dance tutorials with them.

The eighth grade students also created mobile quizzes with a free web resource called Mobile Study (http://mobilestudy.org). As part of their election unit, they developed review quizzes in Mobile Study (they used the classroom computers to create the quizzes). Once the quizzes were complete, they shared them with the other students by sending the quizzes to mobile phones via an Internet link or Bluetooth connection.

The Ninth Graders

The ninth grade students used their mobile phones to develop an inquiry project that was heavily web-based. The project focused on migrant groups in New Zealand. In the past the students had presented their findings on cardboard displays in the classroom. For this project, each student had a blog hosted by Edublogs.com. The blog tracked students' progress and findings on their research projects. Each student also set up an Utterli account. (Utterli was a free web resource that allowed students to record MP3 files from their cell phones and post directly to a blog.) This allowed students to audio record observations and findings and have them instantly post to their edublog. Students could also access and edit their blogs via their mobile phones. With this, the students gained 24/7 access to their on-going projects. Before this project, students only had limited access to the school's computer lab. The students were also able to use YouTube to access videos about migration that they could put right into their blogs via their phones.

The ninth graders initially used the polls on Poll Everywhere to get students to think about migrant groups coming to New Zealand. The teacher set up multiple choice polls asking the students to estimate which migrant group they felt had the largest percentage of migrants to New Zealand last year. Next, the teacher set up a "free text" poll asking students to discuss the results.

The polling allowed all members of the class to participate and to give honest, anonymous feedback that they otherwise might not have shared. Some of the responses gave insight into the way some students felt about the issue and led to a class discussion about the appropriateness of comments and served as a way to approach discussing some prejudice surrounding the topic.

The Twelfth Graders

The twelfth grade students had a class wiki page (created by the teacher at www.wikispaces.com). The teacher wanted to create a co-constructive learning experience for the students where they contributed to the wiki via their mobile phones. The students downloaded Opera Mini on their cell phones so they could easily view the class wiki page. However, the students could not easily contribute to the wiki via their phones, so they ultimately ended up using the school computers.

> ### Hints and Tips from Toni Twiss
>
> Downloading a good mobile browser for accessing the web via cell phone is essential because the default browser on most mobile phones is not particularly user friendly and relies largely on accessing only websites which have been optimized for mobile. A good mobile browser such as Opera Mini will permit any webpage to be viewed on the cell phone (note: this is only for cell phones that can access the mobile web).

The twelfth grade students used a free web-based resource called Qipit, which allowed them to take pictures with their mobile phones that Qipit would turn into PDFs. When the students were brainstorming ideas, they took pictures of their brainstorms and sent them to Qipit, where they were turned them into downloadable PDFs online.

Alternatives

Twiss did not provide an alternative to using mobile phones because every student had access to a phone for the assignments.

School Policies

Most schools in New Zealand ban mobile phones because of teachers' concerns over cheating, distractions, and bullying. Although Twiss works with mobile phones in a variety of schools, almost all of them ban or highly restrict student use of mobile phones on the school campus. Twiss did ask parents to give their consent for their children to participate in the mobile phone activities.

Cell Phone Safety and Etiquette

The students discussed mobile safety before, during, and after the project. The teachers created few new rules; rather, according to Twiss they referred "to the school's Internet safety policy—this was important as students were using the Internet in an unfiltered environment."

Reactions

Twiss found that there were mixed reactions from the students. The older students in Grade 12 were given options to use their cell phones. At first they all were excited to use them, but as they ran into problems with slow Internet access, by the end of the project they had all opted not to use their cell phones. In addition, Twiss felt that older students resented the fact that using the mobile phones made them engage a lot more critically with information and wanted their teacher to go back to providing them with information that had already been established as being accurate or relevant. The teacher also encouraged the students to use their cell phones to search the Internet for information during class activities. Students found it very useful not having to worry about sites that would be blocked as even their class wiki site hosted at Wikispaces (www.wikispaces.com) was blocked at the beginning of the unit. A twelfth grade student said, "I think it was useful that we didn't have blocked sites and we could go on YouTube … because I tried to go on the wiki when we started, but it was blocked and so I couldn't do anything at school so I had to do it all at home." Twiss felt that the novelty of the cell phones was a factor with the older students, and the novelty eventually wore off.

The Grade 8 and 9 students loved the mobile phones. Whereas the twelfth grade students used the phones less and less throughout the project, the younger students came up with more and more ways to use the phones and were regularly asking the teacher to let them use the phones, or suggesting ways that the phones could support them in their learning throughout the day. The ninth grade students liked have the portability of the blogs, so that they could ask the teacher questions at anytime, rather than having to go to the computer lab and bring up the blog on the screen. The ninth graders also liked that they could easily share information and take notes right on their cell phones (rather than writing it down and later putting the information into their blogs).

All the students enjoyed the polling activities with Poll Everywhere and highlighted that they liked the anonymity of the polls, allowing them freedom to respond without concern over being ridiculed or criticized for an incorrect answer.

A twelfth grade teacher describes why she liked using Poll Everywhere: "I really liked the polling thing that we did. You can set up a poll on Poll Everywhere, and the students can text in a response, and then on the screen you can see their answers appearing on the screen. And they can text—you can get thirty responses to the poll and their responses seem to be as long as they want them to be—like we were just getting the kids to text nothing too adventurous—like not an essay or anything but they would get their own responses appearing on the board. They really liked it when their own answer came up and then we copied and pasted it in to Wordle [www.wordle.net], which then created word maps. And all the kids thought that was quite pretty, and I thought that was quite fun. I really enjoyed doing that with them."

Although parents did give consent for their children to be involved, none of the teachers heard from the parents before, during, or after the projects. In all schools, the administration was very supportive of the projects.

Problems

The teachers did encounter some small problems. The ninth grade teacher found that once the students began to have difficulties with using the phones, the teacher had to make more time than she probably would have previously to get students to access computers around the school. This is because once they had begun to struggle with using the Internet on their mobile phones, they needed to have Internet access via computer to finish their projects.

Initially the twelfth grade students took great advantage of using their mobile phones to search the Internet during class for activities. However, by the end of the unit, all students had decided not to use the phones. The students found the phones too slow and too difficult to navigate. Students were also concerned about the lack of "notes" written in to their books for exam preparation as a result of lessons based on co-construction and inquiry.

Unexpected Outcomes

Twiss learned that applications and tools available for use via a mobile phone, including access to the World Wide Web, have a great deal of potential for use in schools. Currently, cost of data is the single biggest factor in limiting this use.

She also found that although teachers are constantly being told that students are "digital natives," many of the students are not as savvy with technology as teachers are led to believe. Though students may seem very "tech savvy," they still need to be taught the skills to deal with the World Wide Web and information overload.

Twiss also learned that professional development was key in helping teachers understand the power of the students' mobile phones. Although it was not part of the class requirement, many ninth grade students said that they began to read the news more often via their phones. The students said they just enjoyed reading the news on their mobile phones, and they often had not paid attention to other news media before (such as television news or newspapers).

Initially, when the students were using the phones to access the Internet, their behavior was extremely collaborative. They were helping each other and sharing web links, but were also discussing the information that they had found and comparing it with that found by others. Even though the students were reading, there was a lot of conversation going on at the same time.

Future Plans

Twiss says, "I don't plan to use mobile phones in a research project form at this stage. However, I continue to work with teachers to develop strategies for their use of student mobile phones in class."

Chapter 2

Case Studies from Math and Science Classrooms

Case Study 11 ▪ **Andrew Douch**

Wanganui Park Secondary College,
Shepparton, Victoria, Australia

Level	Grades 8–12
Subject	Science
Cell Phone Use	Inside and outside the classroom
Cell Phone Activities	Taking photos
Web 2.0 Resources	Poll Everywhere, Utterli, My MiaMia, SMS

The Inspiration

Andrew Douch is the ICT Innovations Leader at Wanganui Park Secondary College, in Shepparton, Victoria, and an Intel Master Trainer. He has been a secondary science teacher for more than 20 years. He has won a number of educational awards for his work with the use of emerging technologies. Douch can be contacted at http://web.mac.com/andrewdouch/.

Douch has always sought new innovations in technology as potential learning tools. He says, "I am keen to use technologies that students already own and find engaging. Mobile phones are a classic example of a technology that you don't have to convince students to use."

School Demographics

Cell Phone Culture

The following describes the cell phone demographics in Douch's classes.

90–95%   of the students had cell phones

Of the students who had cell phones:

100%	could text message and take photos
70–80%	could take and send videos
80–90%	had GPS and/or Bluetooth
20–30%	had mobile Internet

Project Example

Douch describes a text messaging project that he conducted with his astronomy students in 2009 (http://andrewdouch.wordpress.com/2009/04/20/all-abuzz-over-yuri/). "Today in my Astronomy class (year 8) we started learning about space exploration. Students knew who the first person to walk on the moon was, some even knew who the second was. Nobody knew who the first person in space was—although some thought it might have been a Russian. Now, suppose I had simply *told* them who it was. ([whispers] *It was Yuri Gagarin, but shhhhh! because at this point in the story my students don't know that yet.*) How engaging would that have been? Right! It would have been boring and the lesson would have been utterly unmemorable.

"Instead, I told them we were going to have a contest. The first student to get a text message on their phone with the correct answer to the question would be the winner. Students immediately got on their phones and sent messages to anyone they thought would know the answer. There was some nervous waiting for responses and wrong answers, but finally one student won with the right answer.

"The truth is, of course that we were all winners. We'd had fun, learned something—no, not that Yuri Gagarin was the first man in space. Just between us, I don't really think that's terribly important to remember, you can always look it up if you need to know it. The important lesson was in the value of a PLN (personal learning network). If you're reading this blog, you probably realize the value of a PLN in your own career, but how often do we encourage our students to think about cultivating a PLN? In a world where information is voluminous, ubiquitous and free, a person's professional success will not be predicated on an ability to remember facts, but on an ability to quickly access information on the fly. A PLN is powerful for that.

"If *nothing* else, the lesson was memorable. The engagement of students made it a worthwhile novelty—you could see it in their faces. Their pupils were dilated, they were smiling and there was a buzz in the air (literally—from the ringtones)!"

Alternatives

Douch explains, "Well, I guess I could have sent them to the library to look in encyclopedias but that would not have been as engaging, and would have required booking the library—which would have been inconvenient. This was not a major project—but just a way to find out something that we didn't know. So using the tools that the kids already had with them in class, right then in the moment, was much more efficient than booking the library and taking them there next lesson."

School Policies

Student mobile phones were allowed on campus and can be used during class with consent of the teacher.

Cell Phone Safety and Etiquette

Douch spoke to his students before he began the project. He did not give rules. Rather, he says, "I just ask students to behave courteously with their phones the way they should behave courteously with other devices. They should ask themselves, 'Is what I am doing showing respect to the other people here with me?' Whether that is regarding mobile phones, iPods or a pencil—it's not about the tool—it's about the behavior and about showing regard for others."

Reactions

Douch did not hear from parents before, during, or after the projects. He found the students very positive and the administration to be very supportive.

Problems

According to Douch, there were really none to speak of. The students were well behaved. A few of them did not have a mobile phone, or had run out of prepaid credit, so they were not able to participate in the fun directly.

The Domino Effect

A few teachers in Douch's school were using student mobile phones when he began. For example, some math teachers were using them for the calculator. Douch inspired a few new teachers to try using them as well.

Future Plans

"I plan to continue to do the things I already do. What I have done is not really a 'project' per se—just a change in the way things are done. That doesn't end … I just continue to do what works, discard what doesn't, and try new things.

"I'm now using ipadio quite a lot and finding it to be really good. It's a great way to have students make a quick and easy podcast, where the value is in the content and the sharing rather than in production quality."

Case Study 12 ▪ **Jimbo Lamb**

Annville-Cleona Junior-Senior High School,
Annville, Pennsylvania

Level	High School
Subject	Mathematics
Cell Phone Use	Inside and outside the classroom
Cell Phone Activities	Text messaging and phone calling
Web 2.0 Resources	TextMarks, Yodio, Poll Everywhere, Contxts, Drop.io, Google 411

The Inspiration

Jimbo Lamb is a high school mathematics teacher in Pennsylvania. Since fall 2008, Lamb has been using his students' cell phones for a variety of learning activities inside and outside of the classroom. For more information about Lamb, see his blog: http://misterlamb.blogspot.com.

Lamb had an epiphany about the power of cell phones when he was in college. According to Lamb, "Originally, when I was in college, I had sworn off cell phones altogether, thinking to myself that I would never feel the need to be constantly connected, until one night when I was supposed to meet friends at a restaurant, but they changed plans and went elsewhere and had no way to contact me while I was out. When I was out shopping, I realized that I could access a limited Internet through some phones, and decided that if I were to get a phone, it would have to be more than just a phone. Over the years, I became accustomed to having a phone with me, and when the iPhone arrived, I was excited to get one. I waited until the September price drop on the original iPhone and bought one. All of a sudden I had a device that could do so much more than just make phone calls, and with the introduction of the app store, I knew that there had to be a way to include these devices in education."

In the summer of 2008, Lamb attended the National Educational Computing Conference (NECC) in San Antonio Texas. He decided to attend two sessions on ideas for using student cell phones in learning. Once he learned how easy it was to couple websites with cell phones to post and collect data, and that there was no additional cost associated with using many of the web resources, he was determined to try using them with his students.

Lamb first tried using cell phones by conducting text messaging polls with his students using Poll Everywhere (www.polleverywhere.com). Poll Everywhere is a free web resource that couples with cell phones to let users participate in polls via text messaging. Because Poll Everywhere works with any cell phone that has text messaging capabilities, all of Lamb's students' cell phones (basic phones and smartphones) could be used for the activity. At first, when Lamb asked his students to take out their cell phones for a class activity, they did not believe he was being honest with them. Once they started the polling activities, the students were immediately excited by the ability to use their cell phones for a class activity.

School Demographics

Cell Phone Culture

The following describes the cell phone demographics in Lamb's classes.

95% of the students had cell phones

Of the students who had cell phones:

100% could send and receive text messages
90–95% could take pictures
70–80% could take videos
80–90% had GPS and/or Bluetooth
50–60% had mobile Internet access

Social and Economic Data

799 students were enrolled in high school
80% of students pass the statewide reading proficiency
81% of students pass the statewide math proficiency
19% of adults in district have at least a bachelor's degree
87% of adults in district have at least a high school diploma

Economic Status
(from http://schoolmatters.com)

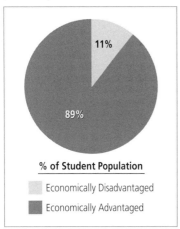

Enrollment by Race/Ethnicity
(from http://schoolmatters.com)

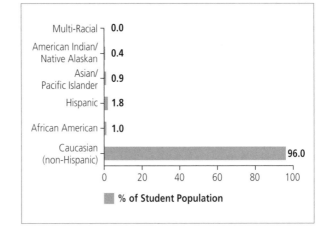

Project Example

Once Lamb had conducted the text messaging polls, he decided to try a larger research project with the aid of cell phones. He asked his Algebra 2 students to complete a research assignment on how quadratics can be applied somewhere in their everyday lives, in something they currently do or in a career they would like to pursue. Because different students would have different interests, he needed an assignment that would allow each student to drive his or her own learning. In addition, he wanted to find a new way to share the information that they found.

Lamb searched the Internet and eventually found Yodio (www.yodio.com). Yodio is a free website that posts audio recordings to the Internet via phone. By a phone call to the Yodio number, an audio recording is made and is immediately posted to a Yodio account as an MP3 file. Once the recordings are on the Yodio website, users can couple pictures with the audio recording to create a digital storybook. Lamb thought this would be the perfect resource for his Algebra 2 project.

Lamb created a Yodio account and began to experiment with the service. Originally, he had his students make a call and enter a PIN number for pulling the recordings into his own account. However, he found this cumbersome. At the same time, Lamb learned that people from Yodio were paying attention to what he was doing in Yodio. He received a contact from Yodio where they offered a free 1-800 number for recording directly to his account so his students did not have to use a PIN and could use a landline if they did not have a cell phone. Yodio told Lamb that they were offering it as a trial, and that if it worked well, he would be able to switch over to a $5 monthly fee to keep the number running, as well as an email address for students to email photos (which could be taken with the students' cell phones and emailed from them) into his account. In the end, he had many quick podcasts that were embedded into his class wiki (http://mrlambmath.wikispaces.com/quadratics) and could be viewed by anyone. Many students told him they were proud of their end product and shared it with friends and family members. One group of students talked about improving a baseball swing with the use of quadratics. Lamb even claimed, "Their insights helped me out in my softball league and in the faculty versus seniors softball game!" Lamb also blogged about his experience (http://misterlamb.blogspot.com/2008/12/cell-phone-exploration-day-1.html).

Alternatives

Lamb did not have to come up with an alternative option for students without cell phones because with the toll-free number, students could use a landline instead of a cell phone to call in their podcasts. Therefore, 100% of his students could participate in the project via landline or cell phone.

School Policies

At Lamb's high school, students are allowed to have cell phones on campus. However, they are not allowed to use them in the classroom during school hours. The cell phones are supposed to be off and out of the teacher's sight during class. Before Lamb began using cell phones in class, he strongly advocated and was able to get a clause in his school's policy that now says, "Cell phones (and iPods/MP3 players) should be turned off and put away unless given permission by the teacher."

As part of Lamb's struggles to get the "phones off unless permission" clause, he had to convince a veteran English teacher that there was a benefit to her. In a summer meeting where they were debating the clause, the English teacher was highly against it, and she came with a thoughtfully prepared speech.

"As she was giving her speech," Lamb told me, "I pulled out my iPhone, accessed the app store, and downloaded the entire works of William Shakespeare for free. When she was done, I slid my phone to her and let her look through it, and she saw all of his works were there. I then asked her how big a book with the same works would be, and whether a student would be able to take it anywhere and everywhere to access it when they want. She conceded that cell phones might be useful in some cases, and the clause was entered into our rules."

Cell Phone Safety and Etiquette

To help his students learn cell phone etiquette, Lamb asked a friend to call him during the middle of a lesson. When the phone rang, and without making an issue out of it, he reached into his pocket and silenced the ring, seamlessly continuing with his lesson as if nothing had happened. After the lesson, Lamb talked about the episode of the ringing phone. His point: Although anyone can make mistakes about leaving ringers on, if a call disrupts a situation, don't panic, and don't make a big deal out of it. Just turn it off and move on. A potential distraction is now something easily dealt with.

Hints and Tips from Jimbo Lamb

Lamb recommends that when teachers begin using cell phones as a learning tool, they should start slowly and keep it simple. Lamb recommends the following:

- Start with an easy activity such as cell phone polling with Poll Everywhere (http://polleverywhere.com). Because most students are very comfortable with text messaging (especially with shows such as *American Idol* where they vote via cell phones), they usually find this an easy activity. There is also instant gratification with the activity because the results show up immediately on the poll.

- Offer alternatives for those without phones (such as Poll Everywhere). "Don't say things like, 'If you don't have a phone … ,' but instead say, 'If you don't have your phone with you … ' You will find that you won't make students feel bad or left out when offering a computer alternative (web voting, podcasting on the computer, etc.).

- Continue to talk about phone etiquette even after you have done a lesson or two on the topic. Throughout the year, teachers should provide examples for students about using their cell phones appropriately. In addition, make sure teachers reward students for proper use of cell phones.

Another activity that Lamb does is to ask his students to bring in a copy of their cell phone bills and plans so they will learn what they can and cannot do on their cell phones. This also helps Lamb understand these limitations and capabilities so he can plan lessons within the boundaries of his students' plans.

Reactions

Overall there has been an incredibly positive reaction from students, parents, and school administrators to Lamb's cell phone activities. Lamb found that his students were excited about the ability to use their cell phones in the classroom. It also seemed to give them a reason to follow the school rules, because they wanted the ability to use the devices throughout the day. When he first used cell phones with a Poll Everywhere quick poll at the beginning of class, he was amazed that when they were done with the poll question, all of the students powered down their phones and put them away. Word got around the school quickly, and by the end of the day, the journalism class was already interviewing Lamb, students, administrators, and other teachers about their views on cell phones in schools for the students' weekly news broadcast!

Lamb had only positive reactions from parents. He says, "So many of the parents were excited about the fact that the cell phones they were paying for were being used for more than just socializing and entertainment. Students were entering their assignments in their calendars, using texting to share ideas and learn. Because I coach soccer, the parents were especially grateful when I created a TextMarks group for updating information, including scores at the end of games that they may not have been able to attend."

Problems

Lamb did not encounter any problems when using cell phones with his students.

Unexpected Outcomes

Lamb felt as though his students' perspectives on cell phones changed greatly— they now understood that their cell phones could be powerful tools for education. During the Yodio Algebra 2 project, Lamb learned that his students were doing everything they would have done had they been writing a report (including writing the report), but because the project involved more than just a written report, the students were more willing to do the necessary work and were proud of their end products.

The Domino Effect

Lamb learned that there were a few other teachers in his school who were interested in using cell phones as a result of his initiative.

Future Plans

Lamb will definitely continue to use cell phones in his teaching. He is working with a different set of students who have a different skill set this year, so the exact plans are still in the works. In addition, his administration is considering more freedom for students to use their phones in school during what would be considered their free time, such as between classes and during lunch.

See Chapter 4, Lesson Plan 1, for a tutorial with Yodio.

Case Study 13 · **Jarrod Robinson**

Boort Secondary College, Victoria, Australia

Level	High School
Subject	Physical Education
Cell Phone Use	Outside and inside the classroom
Cell Phone Activities	Taking photos, text messaging, and recording video
Web 2.0 Resources	Kaywa, SMSExPress.net, Qik, Poll Everywhere, My MiaMia, Mobile Study

The Inspiration

Jarrod Robinson is a physical education and mathematics teacher in Victoria, Australia. Since the beginning of 2008, he has been using his students' mobile phones for mobile activities of polling, audio recording, and most recently QR codes in his physical education and mathematics classrooms. Robinson can be contacted at http://thepegeek.com.

The main reason Robinson chose to start utilizing mobile phones was based on his personal interest in using them in everyday life. "I acknowledged that it had a major role in the organisation of my life, from contacting people through to recording life's moments," he says, "This in itself was enough to have me consider the potential for their use within the classroom. If a mobile phone was important to me, then it sure would be just as important to my students. So why would I deny them the opportunity to use them?"

School Demographics

Social and Economic Data

149 students were enrolled in the school

According to Robinson, "The school population is generally from a low socio-economic background, which one would expect would impact on cell phone ownership. There is a 100% take-up rate among students older than 14."

Project Example

In 2008, Robinson began using mobile phones with his physical education students. He created activities using QR codes with student mobile phones. QR codes ("quick response codes") are "bar codes" for cell phones. They are small square images (like the one shown in Figure 2.1).

Figure 2.1 Sample QR code

On many cell phones you can download free QR code readers (such as at Kaywa) that allow you to use your cell phone camera to take a picture of the QR code, and then receive immediate information on your cell phone. For example, when you take a picture of a QR code, you could receive text, video, an image, an entire novel, a syllabus, a webpage, or a hyperlink with information.

One of the first projects that Robinson developed with QR codes was a GPS scavenger hunt. Robinson created QR code "clues" that students followed around the school. The following is a description of this activity from Robinson's Blog (http://thepegeek.com):

> Today, during lunch time, I helped my students setup QR code readers on their mobile phones in preparation for an activity they will be completing in the coming weeks within my Outdoor Education class. To study the safety aspects and risk taking factors that need to be considered before completing outdoor activities, the students will be completing an orienteering course using their bikes as a form of transportation. However, this is no ordinary course, here's why:

The students will be working in pairs using their mobile phones and their QR code reading software. The course will start with a single QR code; each pair will receive a different code so that they start at a different part of the course.

Students will scan their codes which will then reveal the directions they need to dial into their compasses and a riddle that gives clues as to the location of the first marker and the next QR code.

Halfway throughout the course is a QR code with a difference: it contains a template for an SMS message that links directly to my mobile phone. Once scanned, the students will send a text message that basically asks for the next clue that will then be sent to them so they can complete the course. The final QR code links to a down-loadable Microsoft Word document that details the questions they need to complete around the practical experience as related to the course.

The kids are already super excited about this activity and are looking forward to the challenge of not only deciphering the QR codes, but the riddles contained within them. To generate the QR codes I used the Google generator, then copied them into a word document that you can download here.

However, this time I went around the school with a handheld GPS and marked 12 random locations. I then got 12 of the key questions the students are required to understand and entered them one by one into a QR code generator. Once this was completed, I placed them at the 12 different GPS locations. Now, with this completed, I was finally set up for the activity. The students were then given a blank answer sheet and the GPS location of the first QR code. When they managed to find the code they used their mobile phones to scan and reveal the question that then needed to be answered correctly in order for me to share the next GPS location. This process repeated until they reached the last QR code that included some further information about the assessment piece. The students were also encouraged to utilize their MP3 players to listen to their audio workbooks and podcasts of key content if they were unsure of an answer.

Beyond his physical education classes, Robinson now has started to integrate QR codes into his math worksheets. He creates a QR code that is loaded with extra information about what is on the worksheet (such as a YouTube video, an audio feed, a picture, or a helpful website). This allows his students to get extra help or extend the learning on a basic worksheet. Students scan the code with their cell phones (take a picture) and receive the relevant information on their phones.

Robinson also takes advantage of his students' interest in SMS text messaging by using text messaging to help his students prepare for exams and homework activities. In the days prior to the exam, he schedules text messages to be delivered to his students' cell phones at designated times. These messages ask the students to employ a series of higher-order thinking skills such as synthesis or evaluation. This allows his students to be more focused, helping them to synthesize a stronger answer from the information they are given.

Robinson also has developed quizzes for his students' mobile phones with an online resource called Mobile Study (http://mobilestudy.org). Mobile Study allows you to create quizzes online and then distribute them to cell phones, where students can take the quiz.

Alternatives

Robinson will often pair up students to work together, so not everyone has to own a phone. He has found that partnering students "puts no pressure on those students who don't have access. Another alternative is to make a call out for parents to donate old mobile phones that would usually be thrown out. This makes it possible to have a class set of phones."

School Policies

Robinson explains that currently, "Our school policy is supportive of mobile phones. Up until my introduction of mobile phones in the classroom, they were very much blacklisted. However, after staff training and pressure from the students, we are now supportive of their use within the classroom as long as it is under teacher direction and appropriate to the task at hand."

Hints and Tips from Jarrod Robinson

Robinson recommends to begin using cell phones "with an anonymous survey to obtain information about how many of your students have access to their own personal mobile phone. This survey could also help you work out what features students have on their phones and will assist you in planning for their inclusion in your curriculum. With this information, you can decide to move forward with the introduction. For example, if it turns out that only 5% of your students have access, then logic would tell you not to bother. It would also stop you from running an activity that required GPS access to work out that no students actually have a GPS-enabled phone. It pays to do your background homework."

Reactions

Robinson has found increased motivation from both his students and parents as a result of using mobile phones in his classroom. He explains, "Students have embraced the use of the technologies they love within their learning. It has motivated them to complete assessments and homework that may or may not have been completed using traditional approaches. Parents have also enjoyed learning the new ways of communication at school and as such have participated in parent information nights focused on explaining the process and reasoning behind the push to use mobiles within the classroom."

Problems

Robinson did not find any problems with the students using their phones inappropriately; rather, he had problems with the school's policy on mobile phone use. He explains, "Initial problems were based on the fact that access wasn't allowed at school so I had to get personal approval from the principal in order to allow me to utilise them within the classroom. Students also thought that it was some sort of trick when I asked them to bring and use their phones in class."

The Domino Effect

According to Robinson, "A few teachers within my subject area have also got interested in utilizing mobile phones in their classes—starting simply with using them as one-to-one video cameras, MP3 players, and so on. They have also enjoyed communicating with their students in the after hours via bulk messaging."

Future Plans

Robinson continues to use mobile phones often with his students. His plans include "more of a rollout into communication with parents' phones, which would include things such as sending reporting information. I would also be interested in seeing all staff at my school utilizing the SMS bulk messaging service."

Case Study 14 ▪ **Rebekah Randall**

Huron High School, Ann Arbor, Michigan

Level	High School (Grade 12)
Subject	Physics
Cell Phone Use	Outside the classroom
Cell Phone Activities	Taking photos
Web 2.0 Resources	None

The Inspiration

Rebekah Randall is in her fourth year as a high school physics teacher in Ann Arbor, Michigan.

Although she never had any inclination to use her students' cell phones in physics, she found that her students took the initiative on their own during a physics trip to a local amusement park. As a result, Randall learned about how the "toys" in her students' pockets could become productive tools for documenting physics experiences.

School Demographics

Cell Phone Culture

The following describes the cell phone demographics in Randall's classes.

90–95%   of her twelfth graders have their own cell phones

Of the students who had cell phones:

100%   could send and receive text messages
100%   could send and receive photos

Social and Economic Data

Huron High School is a high achieving public school that is fairly diverse socioeconomically.

2100   students were enrolled in the high school
83%   of students pass the statewide reading proficiency
73%   of students pass the statewide math proficiency
96%   of adults in district have at least a high school diploma
69%   of adults in district have at least a bachelor's degree

Economic Status
(from http://schoolmatters.com)

Enrollment by Race/Ethnicity
(from http://schoolmatters.com)

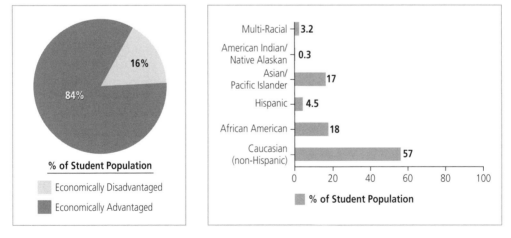

Project Example

Randall decided that instead of another multiple-choice test for a final exam, she wanted her physics students to do a large project based on experiencing roller coasters at a local amusement park. In essence, the field trip was a large lab. Students were required to keep a record of this experience that included pictures of the roller coasters.

The rubric for this project lists "A title page that states the principle that you are testing and the ride it is being tested on and any appropriate graphics you want to include."

Although the original idea was for her students to download pictures of the roller coasters from the Internet when they were back in class, during the field trip Randall noticed many of the students using their own cell phones to take pictures at the park. She was surprised and delighted that some of pictures were used for their lab reports. Inclusion of this real-time material made the report and the whole process that much more authentic an experience for the students.

Alternatives

Because Randall did not originally plan on using cell phones during the project, she had not developed an alternative for students without cell phones. Her original assignment stated that students could use pictures of amusement park rides that they found on Google. Although this was less authentic, it was Randall's initial plan.

Hints and Tips from Rebekah Randall

Be open to the new devices of your students! Randall has allowed a student here or there to use a cell phone in class when they have asked. Some students have used it as a calculator, though not during testing situations, and occasionally students have used cell phones to look up information on the Internet when it related to a class project. She has classes of around 10 students and is able to keep a very careful watch over individual instances of cell phone use to make this a viable solution. One worry that many teachers at her new school have is that one of the students will use the advanced functions of their cell phones as translators (to look up answers for class tests and quizzes), and this use is banned during the school day.

School Policies

The policy at Randall's high school is that cell phones are allowed on campus but cannot be seen or heard in class. Randall did not have to worry about her school's policy affecting the project, because students were only using their cell phones off campus to document their physics labs.

Cell Phone Safety and Etiquette

Randall had not discussed cell phone safety or etiquette with her students, because she had not originally planned on using their cell phones for the project. Before the field trip, cell phone numbers of the teachers were given to the students for emergency purposes, and when one student did not arrive back on the bus in a timely fashion, another student was able to contact the missing student via cell phone. Although cell phone use was not a part of the class project, it certainly helped with the effectiveness and safety of the field trip.

Reactions

Randall's high school students were delighted to be able to use their own images for their lab reports rather than ones they found on the Internet. It made the project much more authentic to the students.

Problems

There were none! Because students were not required to use their cell phones, only students who took the initiative used cell phones to take pictures for their lab reports.

Unexpected Outcomes

Students' spontaneous and creative use of their cell phones in this project was the biggest unexpected outcome. Randall found that allowing students to take and use their own images made the projects more authentic to her students.

Future Plans

Randall says, "I will seriously consider expanding the use of cell phones next year after I get a better feeling for the school and the expected classroom environment. I will have fewer than 15 students per class, so I should be able to accurately gauge the interest in this technology. I plan on taking my freshmen outside as much as I can while there is good weather. Integrating cell phones into an outdoor lab experience will be a fun challenge."

See Chapter 4, Lesson Plan 10, for a lesson plan and tutorial on sending pictures to the web via cell phone.

Case Study 15 ▪ **Kipp Rogers**

Mary Passage Middle School, Newport News, Virginia

Level	Middle School (Grades 6–8)
Subject	Math
Cell Phone Use	Inside and outside the classroom
Cell Phone Activities	Taking photos, using phone as a calculator, text messaging
Web 2.0 Resources	Poll Everywhere, Google SMS, Blogger, Wiffiti

The Inspiration

Kipp Rogers is both a principal and a math teacher at Mary Passage Middle School in Newport News, Virginia. Not only has Rogers taught a math class where he encouraged his students to use their cell phones, but in his leadership position as a school principal he encouraged other teachers to try out their students' cell phones for a variety of activities including blogging, polling, organizing, dictionaries, calculating, and podcasting.

Two years ago, the middle school ran out of calculators for a schoolwide math exam. Having 850 students and only 500 calculators, after the school searched all over to find more, they were still short. Rogers explains, "I was teaching a math class at the time and was two calculators short. I told one of my students to use the calculator on the PALM Trio I had then. The student indicated that he had a calculator on his cell phone but had never used it. I asked the other student without a calculator if she had a cell phone. She did; it was in her locker. I told them both to get their phones from their lockers." Rogers found that his students were excited to be able to use their phones in the open for school. As a result, he began to research other uses of the students' cell phones in learning.

School Demographics

Cell Phone Culture

The following describes the cell phone demographics in Rogers' classes.

70–80%   of the students had cell phones

Of the students who had cell phones:

100%	could send text messages
90–95%	could take and send photos
80%	had Bluetooth or GPS options
20–30%	had access to mobile Internet

Social and Economic Data

850	students were enrolled in the middle school
73%	of students pass the statewide reading proficiency
64%	of students pass the statewide math proficiency

The per capita income of the district (from 2009) was about $23,454.

Economic Status
(from http://schoolmatters.com)

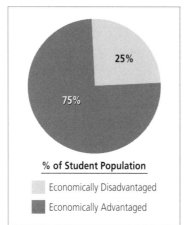

Enrollment by Race/Ethnicity
(from http://schoolmatters.com)

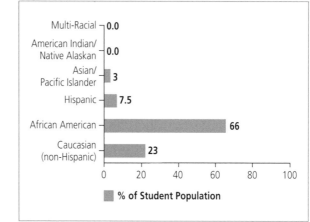

Project Example

Initially, Rogers used cell phones as a means to encourage students to do their work with an activity called "phone Fridays." Rogers was not certain that using cell phones would enhance curriculum learning, but he knew it could be engaging to some of his less motivated students. Therefore, he sent a permission slip home to parents to let them know what their children would be doing with their cell phones in the classroom. Rogers said that almost immediately the students began to think of ideas and ways to use their cell phones in an educative way, such as taking pictures of the notes on the whiteboard, or using the cell phone calendar to help organize their own schedules. In addition to calculators, students also used the stopwatch feature on their cell phones for math-related activities, created podcasts, and even blogged with their cell phones for homework.

Soon after, Rogers was speaking with fellow educator Sheryl Nuessbaum Beach, who was familiar with Cellphonesinlearning.com (the author's website) and recommended that he look there to find out how he could better connect using cell phones to student learning, and not just as a motivating tool.

At first, Rogers and his students were quietly doing these cell phone activities behind the closed doors of his classroom. Once he saw the positive student reactions and excitement, he decided to share his ideas on using cell phones with the other teachers at his middle school. He found five teachers who were enthusiastic to pilot using the student cell phones in their teaching. Nervous about inappropriate student use, the teachers came up with a set of norms around using the cell phones in the classroom. Each teacher talked about the norms with the students and enforced the rules. The teachers asked their students for their ideas concerning cell phone usage in the classroom and found that the students came up with a very similar set of norms.

To begin, the goal was to "get kids excited" about using their cell phones. Next, a survey [for an example of a student mobile literacy survey, see "Survey Students" in Chapter 5] was sent home to encourage a conversation between parents and their children about their cell phone plans. Then, students spent time coming up with classroom rules around appropriate use of cell phones (based on their earlier discussion of norms of cell phone use). The rules included only talking on cell phones to complete assignments in classroom; only sending text, pictures, or videos with permission from teacher; no recording video, audio, or pictures of people without permission; no posting to online websites without permission; and practicing online safety when publishing from a cell phone.

Rogers said, "We spent a lot of time talking about digital literacy and digital footprints. Sometimes with middle school children, they don't get the end result of what they are doing, and that things can be traced back to the original creator of the media." In the end, the teachers set up a box in the front of the room where they would sometimes ask students to put their cell phones when they were not being used during class time.

Being the principal, Rogers was able to help change the school's policy to include student cell phones for learning activities. The teachers began using the cell phones for simple activities such as polling with Poll Everywhere or Google SMS to do research. They slowly began to add new activities as they and the students became comfortable with each new activity.

Rogers concluded, "Many teachers are now using the cell phones with Blogger. com. Some, especially English teachers, have been creating photostories with student cell phones. English teachers at Passage Middle School are using blogs as one way to engage their students in the writing process. Cell phones have been a welcome addition, as the students now take pictures with their cell phones outside of school, post them to their blogs, and then they write new posts on their blogsf about the picture. At the same time the teachers have been very careful to not make the cell phone the lead attraction or lead actor in the play, rather just the tool to gather or produce the data or research."

These activities not only meet the school's requirement for encouraging students to write more, but also give students an opportunity to connect their everyday world with their in-class writing activities by using an authentic image related to the writing.

A few other examples of new applications by staff include teachers using Wiffiti (an interactive blank text messaging board online) with homework. At this site, students can post questions they have concerning homework assignments and activities. One teacher used student cell phones for silent Socratic seminars. In this format, the teacher can pose questions back and forth via text rather than verbally. Another teacher is using Twitter as a form to generate stories in the class.

Alternatives

Because not all of his students have cell phones, Rogers encouraged the use of sharing cell phones as well as using web resources that had alternatives to cell phone use (such as web options and toll-free numbers).

School Policies

Rogers's school policy is very progressive compared to most other cases in this chapter because it allows cell phones on campus that can be used during class only for instructional purposes. Being an administrator, Rogers was aware of the pitfalls of allowing students to use their own cell phones in school. Consequently, he chose to work with students, faculty, and administrators to develop this inclusive acceptable-use policy. The policy states the appropriate and inappropriate uses of student cell phones during school hours. Figure 2.2 on the following page shows the policy form that students and their parents must sign.

Cell Phone Safety and Etiquette

Rogers and his teachers all agreed that before they began using student cell phones, they needed to spend some time discussing issues of digital footprints with the students. According to Webopedia (2011), "On the Internet a digital footprint is the word used to describe the trail, traces or 'footprints' that people leave online. This is information transmitted online, such as forum registration, emails and attachments, uploading videos or digital images and any other form of transmission of information—all of which leaves traces of personal information about yourself available to others online." Rogers and the teachers wanted the students to understand the consequences of cell phone posting to the Internet, as well as cell phone messaging to friends and others.

Reactions

"The excitement level of the kids when they came into class to find out what they were going to be doing with the cell phones was just phenomenal," says Rogers. "The students have been very enthusiastic. When doing projects, we never had students say, 'I left my phone at home.' Students also shared their phones nicely when others did not have them. Many times that was due to parents taking them away as punishment."

Rogers has not heard from many parents, although he says, "I did have one parent ask me why their child had to get a cell phone for their English class. I laughed and explained what the teacher was doing in class. She thought it was a great idea."

Figure 2.2 Mary Passage Middle School Cell Phone Policy

Student's Name _____

1. Students will talk on their cell phones only to complete assignments that are related to the instructional lesson.

2. Students will keep cell phones turned off or left in lockers when they are not being used for instructional purposes in class.

3. Students will only send text messages, pictures or video messages to others outside of the classroom with permission and directions from the teacher.

4. Students will not record still or moving images or voices of students or the teacher without permission from the teacher.

5. Students will not post recordings of still or moving images or voice recordings of students or the teacher to online websites without their permission.

6. Students will practice Internet safety with online resources.

7. Students will post only appropriate text, audio, and visual media to online websites.

I _____ understand that violation of our class acceptable cell phone use policy may result in my not being able to participate in additional class activities that involve using the cell phone. I also understand that I may receive disciplinary consequences for violating school board policies regarding cyber-bullying.

I _____ have gone over the Cell Phones in Class Acceptable Use Policy with my child and agree to allow my child to participate.

Parent's signature _____

Student's signature _____

Teacher's signature _____

Problems

Although there were problems with student cell phones before Rogers implemented the new rules for learning, after two years of using the cell phones for learning, Rogers has not encountered any discipline or management problems with cell phones being used for that purpose.

Rogers does think that using a device that is always in his students' pockets cut down on missing homework and forgetfulness. "Not one time when we used cell phones did I ever have a kid tell me that he forgot his homework!" He found that especially for middle schoolers, who often struggle with organization, teaching them how to effectively use their cell phones for organization and data collection has given them a lifelong management tool.

Hints and Tips from Kipp Rogers

- Start simple with something you can easily control, like using the calculators on the cell phones.

- Let the kids get involved in suggesting ideas on how to couple learning with their cell phones.

Unexpected Outcomes

Rogers learned that although the socioeconomic background of his inner-city students is quite diverse, the one device they all have in common is a cell phone. Whereas the type of cell phone that students own may differ, they all have some basic functions that can be useful in learning. As a matter of fact, Rogers found that many of his parents do not even have landlines, and thus using a cell phone to communicate with parents is often a more direct and accessible route.

As a result, Rogers has started communicating with parents via Twitter (he tweets), and he uses TextMarks to blast his parents with information about school-related activities. This provides his parents with multiple forms of communication to get the same message. "I think it helps me stay in touch with parents better," he says, "Especially those busy parents who appreciate the 'just in time' information. For example, when the flu shot was being offered, the parents found out via text message and then could come over to the school to receive their shots that day."

Rogers found that the level of engagement with work that takes place in the classroom has greatly increased. Students are more apt to do homework that allows them to use their cell phones. The cell phones are there to support good instruction. Teachers do not develop assignments specifically for the cell phone; rather, they bring in the cell phone to aid with the assignments when it is deemed useful.

The Domino Effect

Because Rogers is the principal of the school, he is in a position to advocate and help his teachers find effective and appropriate ways to use cell phones in their classrooms. Thus, many teachers in every subject area at his middle school have started using cell phones in their teaching.

In addition, he is inspiring other teachers in his school district. A fifth grade teacher at the local elementary school is using cell phones as part of his center activities, to help introduce cell phones as a learning tool to the students before many of them receive their own cell phones!

Future Plans

Rogers has many future plans for using student cell phones in his middle school. "We have expanded our scope because we have had more time to experiment and research specific activities that coordinate with our curriculum. Primarily we will be using the cell phones with blogging. The possibilities cross all subjects and provide a great vehicle to reinforce higher-order thinking and writing."

For professional development in fall 2009, he had all of his teachers learn how to microblog using their cell phones and Twitter. He had them attend a feature film in the theater, and tweet via their cell phones their reactions to different parts of the movie. It was an exercise in discourse and language, to show his teachers the power of being able to microblog in real-time.

See Chapter 4, Lesson Plan 10, for a lesson plan and tutorial on sending pictures and media to a blog via cell phone.

Case Study 16 ▪ **Lynne Sullivan**

Cranbrook Upper School, Bloomfield Hills, Michigan

Level	High School
Subject	Science (Chemistry)
Cell Phone Use	Inside and outside the classroom
Cell Phone Activities	Text messaging, phone calls
Web 2.0 Resources	Drop.io, Gabcast, Gcast

The Inspiration

Lynne Sullivan has been teaching at Cranbrook Upper School for the past three years. She teaches high school chemistry.

In 2007–08 Sullivan was a student in the Masters and Certification program at the University of Michigan. In her teacher education technology course taught by the author, she was exposed to different ways in which cell phones could be used for learning. Sullivan stayed open to the fact that using student cell phones might be a handy tool for her one day. In addition, she believed that all kids loved their cell phones and would probably rather use them than take notes the traditional way. Therefore, she was on the lookout for the best opportunity to take advantage of these tools so that they would improve student learning. She started using student cell phones in 2008 during a science museum field trip.

School Demographics

Cell Phone Culture

The following describes the cell phone demographics in Sullivan's classes.

100% of the students had cell phones

Of the students who had cell phones:

100% could send text messages
70–80% could take and send photos

Social and Economic Data

According to the Cranbrook Schools website, "Cranbrook Schools is a private college prep boarding school located in Bloomfield Hills, Michigan, near Detroit. Cranbrook is comprised of three schools: an elementary school with a private preschool, a middle school with a distinct boys middle school and girls middle school along with a co-ed college prep private boarding high school."

During the time of this case study there were 780 students in the Upper School, 255 of whom were boarders. These students came from 17 states and 15 countries, reflecting a diversity of races, ethnic origins, and religious beliefs.

The Project(s)

During a visit to the Cranbrook Institute of Science, Sullivan asked students to take photos of minerals or elements with their cell phones. Pictures were uploaded to Drop.io. Students without the ability to take photos with their phones were given the option of recording a "podcast" message with their phones on Drop.io. Figure 2.3 shows a copy of the assignment.

Alternatives

Sullivan did not include any alternatives because 100% of her students owned cell phones and were able to use them for the project.

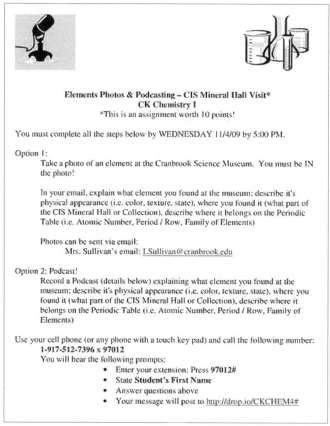

Figure 2.3 Chemistry class assignment

School Policies

Student cell phones are allowed on campus and can be used during class only for instructional purpose. Because policy permits this use, administration did not need to be informed about the specifics of this project.

Cell Phone Safety and Etiquette

Sullivan did not discuss cell phone safety and etiquette because the school has a policy for technology use in place that she expects them to follow.

Reactions

Sullivan found that her students seemed to like it. It was a limited event, and she would like to expand this type of use further.

Problems

There were none.

> **Hints and Tips from Lynne Sullivan**
>
> Sullivan advocates that other teachers
> "Just try it!"

The Domino Effect

Sullivan does not think any other teachers were inspired to start using cell phones.

Future Plans

Sullivan intends to continue using cell phones in her classroom. She is planning on using them "as a feedback tool for a group project where students develop their own conceptual physics labs."

Chapter 3

Cell Phone Use for School Administration

This chapter considers how teachers and administrators are currently using cell phones for management and other administrative duties. Cell phones allow students, parents, teachers, administrators, and community members another access point to schoolwide information. For example, board meetings can be live streamed to the Internet as well as to cell phones via a free Internet resource called Qik. Text message alerts can be used to reach groups and subgroups of parents and committee members. The following are a few free or low cost mobile resources that can be helpful for school administration.

Dial2Do

http://Dial2Do.com

Dial2Do is a free (for 30 days) speech-to-text phone application. Once you register online, you can select the activities you wish to do with Dial2Do. For example, you can select to send a text message, send an email, post to a Google Calendar, post to a blog, translate language, listen to email, listen to a calendar entry, set reminders, and much more. All of these activities can be done with one phone call to the Dial2Do number. If you wish to send a text message, call Dial2Do and respond to "What would you like to do?" Say "text," and the name of the person or group to whom you want to send a text message, and then record the message. Dial2Do will transcribe the speech to text and send the text message! You will also receive an archive of all the messages and posts that you create in a private Dial2Do account (both audio and text versions are available). Dial2Do is an excellent way for students, teachers, and administrators to create their own digital planners or organizers. Students could call in to set up reminders for assignments, listen to the class calendar, post a blog reflection, text, email their group members or their teachers, or listen to news feeds. Teachers and administrators to could use Dial2Do to send mass text or email alerts. With one phone call, they could send and receive reminders, write blog posts, organize and keep track of finances for the budget, post assignments and activities to the class web calendar, and more. Lesson Plan 6 in Chapter 4 is a tutorial on Dial2Do.

Kaywa

www.kaywa.com

Kaywa is a website that allows anyone to create QR codes. (QR codes are quick response codes, a bar code for cell phones.) Using a QR code reader on your cell phone (which you can download for free from Kaywa), you can take a picture of a QR code and immediately you will receive information on your phone associated with that QR code (it could be text, or a picture, a web link, an email address, or even a movie!). At Kaywa, it is very easy to create your own QR code. Once it has been created you can post it on the Internet, put it on a digital document, or print it off and use it on a hard copy. Teachers can use Kaywa to create QR codes for their class syllabi, handouts, permission forms, homework help, or weekly homework assignments. Students or parents can take a picture of the code and receive all the information associated with that code on their phones. Lesson Plan 9 in Chapter 4 is a tutorial on Kaywa.

Pulse.to

http://pulse.to

Pulse.to is a free web resource that allows users to create their own keyword alerts for sending mass text messages. The text message alerts can be sent from the Pulse.to website or from a cell phone. You can also set up multiple alerts for different groups of people in Pulse.to. Therefore, an administrator or teacher can sign up for a free account in Pulse.to and then use it to send alerts to groups of people (parents, committee members, teachers, staff, students). Kipp Rogers, a middle school principal, began using text alerts in 2009. He sends schoolwide alert messages for parents and community members. Following is the signup that the parents and community members use.

> **Text Alerts:** To keep updated, subscribe to TextMarks to receive alerts (text messages) on your mobile phone as soon as I send them! Just send a text message to 41411 with SUBSCRIBE PASSAGE in it, or subscribe online.

Jimbo Lamb, a high school math teacher, is using cell phones increasingly in different ways in his classroom management. During the 2009–10 school year, to help facilitate the daily assignments, Lamb used TextMarks (which is not free, but you could use Pulse.to instead) each day to update the most current assignment and remind students of upcoming assessments. Lamb says, "Many of the parents were excited about the fact that the cell phones they were paying for were being use for more than just socializing and entertainment. Students were entering their assignments in their calendars, using texting to share ideas and learn, etc."

Lamb is also a soccer coach and has used text alerts through TextMarks to update parents about the progress of the game. This allowed parents who were not able to attend the game to learn about the game activities in the moment.

Twitter (mobile)

http://twitter.com

Administrators or teachers could set up a school (or class) Twitter account. Using the Twitter feed (and their cell phones), they could post live announcements in the moment. Parents could subscribe to the feed (via mobile or web) to get the latest updates. Middle school principal Kipp Rogers set up a schoolwide Twitter account (http://twitter.com/passagems). The purpose of this account was to allow parents, students, and community members to easily subscribe to the Twitter feed (via web or cell phone). Because Rogers carries his cell phone with him at all times, he is able to send tweets from his cell phone directly to the Twitter feed to update in the moment. This allows him to get school information out instantly and alert people to any immediate changes in the schedule or daily activities. Instead of running back to his office computer, he can use his readily available cell phone without interrupting his day to find a computer to compose the message. Paul Wood uses Twitter for his office hours. Each night for a designated time, he makes himself available to his students via Twitter (or just a simple text message on his phone).

Flickr (mobile)

http://flickr.com

Administrators can create a Flickr video and photo sharing account for the school (similar to the White House Flickr feed, www.flickr.com/photos/whitehouse). They can select who will be allowed to post cell phone pictures and videos to the feed (it could be limited to themselves, teachers, journalism students, etc.). Teachers could also create mobile feeds for their class or club activities, such as the drama club posting pictures from the school musical.

Qik

http://qik.com

Qik is a free online resource that allows users to stream video live from their cell phones to the Internet. For example, teachers could stream their classes directly to the web. This would allow homebound students or students who are unable to be in class for other reasons to stay up to date on class activities. In addition, parents could watch and learn how to help their children with homework. Jarrod Robinson (Case Study 13) has set up a Qik account (http://qik.com/mrrobbo) so that he can project his students' learning to the Internet, where parents can peek in on the learning activities!

Google Voice

http://google.com/voice

Google Voice is a free application that allows anyone to sign up and receive a free local phone number. Google voice is a private web-based voicemail system with many features. It can transcribe speech to text for any and all voicemails. Every voicemail left in your Google Voice account automatically becomes an MP3 file that can be downloaded or used anywhere on the web. In Google Voice online, you can send text messages or make phone calls. Further, you can create unique greetings for individuals or specific groups of callers. For example, a teacher can create a group for parents, then they can select this group when they need to send out a mass text message. Google Voice also allows you to record phone conversations as they are happening (as long as the caller called using your Google Voice phone number). Teachers and administrators can set up Google Voice in order to hand out the Google Voice number rather than their personal cell phone numbers. They can set any phone(s) to ring when the Google Voice number is called (for example, the office phone, home phone, Skype, or a cell phone). This allows for many ways to reach administrators or teachers with one number. In addition, teachers or administrators can use the live phone call recording feature to archive any parent calls, conferencing, or other important calls. All messages (audio and text) are archived in Google Voice so that there is a running record of communication. Lesson Plan 2 in Chapter 4 is a tutorial on Google Voice.

Remind101

www.remind101.com

Remind101 is a free site created for teachers and students to seamlessly create text and/or email reminders for assignments, projects, quizzes, tests, labs, class activities and homework. Teachers create accounts, upload syllabi, insert all class projects, activities, homework and assignments. Then students can log in to Remind101, search for their class, subscribe to the class, and automatically start receiving all reminders for the class activities. Students can add new reminders, or personalize the text alerts to be for only certain types of activities. One of the best aspects of this site is that it is quick and easy to use. Instructors can also use the same class site over and over again, just changing the due dates. The site works with any cell phone that has SMS text messaging!

Basic Text Messaging and Phone Calls

Many of the teachers in this book use text messaging and phone calls to communicate with students and/or parents. The teachers often set structures around the times that the students are allowed to contact their teachers. For example, Judy Pederson (Case Study 7) often uses text messaging to communicate with her students. She gives out her cell phone number and allows her students to text (or call) any time until 9:00 p.m. to ask for clarification on an assignment. She also sends out homework and study reminders to her students by this mechanism.

Administrator Lesson Plan 1

Now Hear This!
Cross-Posting Announcements via Pixelpipe

About Pixelpipe

Pixelpipe (http://pixelpipe.com) allows anyone to send a piece of media from a cell phone to a large number of places online with a single text message. For example, if you take a picture of the school play, you can send the picture to the school Twitter, Flickr, Blogger, and Facebook accounts. With one account, you can post from any phone. Therefore, superintendents, principals, and teachers can update the school announcements.

Lesson Description

Administrators will learn how to cross-post all school announcements from their cell phones to to the many networking sites they use to disseminate information. For example, the principal can use his or her cell phone to send a photo of the school speaker to the school's Flickr photo feed, the school blog, and the school Facebook page all at the same time from one text message.

Process

Before beginning, create accounts (if you don't already have them) on the third-party sites (e.g., Flickr, Twitter, Facebook, blog) that you will use for posting.

  1. Go to http://pixelpipe.com and sign up for an account.

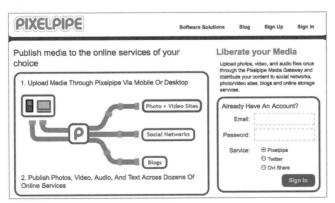

The signup/login screen for Pixelpipe

2. Click on *Add Pipes*.

3. In Add Pipes, you can select the third-party sites that you would like to cross-post to.

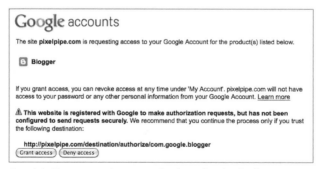

Choose your pipes—third-party applications—from the list provided

4. When you select a "pipe," you're told what types of mobile applications can post there (e.g., text, video, photos). In addition, you are asked to sign in to that account and approve the posting (for example, the next figure shows Blogger asking the user to sign in to her Blogger account to approve the posting).

Google's Blogger requires you to log in and authorize it to accept Pixelpipe postings

5. Then Pixelpipe will ask if you want to send directly from your phone to the third-party site when you send to Pixelpipe from your phone.

6. Next, click on *Settings*. In Settings, you are given an "Upload by Email" address that you can use to upload from your cell phone. You should add a new contact in your cell phone and put the email address in it.

7. Now when you want to send a picture, text, or video to multiple places on the Internet from one mobile message, you can do so by sending the media to the Pixelpipe email address in your phone. The media will automatically show up on all the sites selected in Pixelpipe.

Extensions

- Pixelpipe could also be used for student learning with journalism students. Students could document their local news reporting in multiple places, just as real reporters do. Pixelpipe is a great way to report the news.

Administrator Lesson Plan 2

Text Alerting via Joopz

About Joopz

Joopz (http://joopz.com) is a free web-based system to send and receive text messages via the web. Text messages can be sent to one person or a group of people. Joopz archives the messages sent (although you do need to become a premium member for about $19.95 a year, the rate from 2011, to keep long-term text message communication archives).

Lesson Description

Administrators or teachers could use Joopz to communicate school alerts, or target teacher, parent, and committee communications via text message. All the communication is archived in Joopz. All participants can reply and have two-way communication via text message. You can work from the Joopz website or your cell phone. In addition, you can choose to let members of different school groups communicate with each other via Joopz messaging.

Process

1. Go to http://joopz.com and sign up.

2. Once an account has been created, you can add contacts by clicking on *Contacts* and adding new contacts and their cell phone numbers.

Adding contacts and groups in Joopz

3. Once the contacts are added, you can create Groups (this is helpful if you want to send a mass text message to multiple people at once). Notice that in Groups, you have a choice to create a Broadcast Group (where only you receive the reply messages from group members) or a Chat Group (where all the members will receive a reply message).

4. Once you have contacts and groups created, you can send messages. Click on *Messages* and send up to a 100-character message to an individual or group. In addition, you can set a specific time to send the message. For example, if you want it to be sent just at the end of the school day, but are worried that you will forget, simply set it up beforehand.

The Joopz message screen allows you to send to groups and individuals and to set many options

5. If someone sends a message back, it will appear in the Joopz Messages (or you can turn on SMS forwarding and have it delivered directly to your own cell phone). All of the messages will show up in the Messages page.

Administrator Lesson Plan 3

Opt-in School Alert System via Celly

About Celly

Celly (http://cel.ly) is a mass text messaging service that allows you to set up a shortcode keyword so people can easily join your text alert service. Therefore, an administrator or teacher can sign up for a free account in Celly and then use it to send alerts to groups of people (parents, committee members, teachers, staff, students, etc.). Then people can begin to join your text alert by sending the administrator's account shortcode to the Celly number (23559). You can get started by texting "start" to 23559. Celly will ask you for a login and password. You then go to the Celly website, login, and set up text message channels. Each channel is set up with a keyword so that people can join your mass text message with a keyword from their cell phone! There does not seem to be a limit on the number of people that can join your mass alert. Celly gives you three choices in how you want to set up the mass text alerts: (1) chat, where all members can send messages back and forth to the whole group, (2) alert, where only the teacher (owner of the channel) sends messages to the group, or (3) feedback, where group members send messages back to the teacher only. In addition, your texting channel can be public or private. All messages are archived in Celly. You can send messages via the Celly website or via phone call. It works quickly and easily.

Lesson Description

An administrator (or teacher) will set up a Celly alert system for the school. It is an "opt in" system where the administrator will choose a keyword that all students and/or parents can send a text message to in order to subscribe to the alert system. By creating an "opt in" system, the school can avoid having to type in all cell phone numbers of all community members. In addition, the school does not have to worry about sending a text to someone who does not want them or cannot afford them.

Process

1. Sign up in Celly by texting "Start" to 23559. You will be asked for a password.

2. Login to http://Cel.ly and sign in to your account (click on *Login*)

Celly Welcome screen

3. Create a keyword shortcode (make sure it is one that is easy to remember and related to the school) by clicking on *Start a Channel*.

4. Add the channel name (keyword) and a welcome message. Select a channel type (Chat, Alert, or Feedback), which designates how you want to set up the mass text alerts. Then select the level of privacy (Invite Only, Password, Public). Click on *Create Channel*.

Channel Name:

smithschool

Channel names are unique across Celly like usernames. They must be one word (no spaces), using normal letter characters, and must be between 6 and 20 characters.

Welcome Message:

Welcome to Smith High School Alert System

People will see this welcome message when they join your channel. Max 140 characters.

Channel Type:

◉ **Chat (default)**

○ **Alert**

○ **Feedback**

Privacy:

◉ **Invite Only (default)**

○ **Password:**

○ **Public**

Create Channel

Start a Channel screen

5. You can invite participants either by email or by keyword (via text messaging). Under Actions you can click on "Invite people to #channel." When the invite window opens up you will see how to invite people via email or they can send in the keyword to 23559!

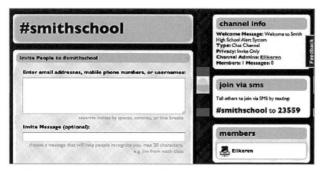

Inviting participants to the channel

6. You can send an alert to all the subscribers by typing in the message box and selecting then clicking *Send*. You can also send an alert from your phone by sending a text to 23559 and in the text #channelname and then your message. All the group members can also log in to Celly and send messages via the web (or via text message if you set up a Chat or Feedback channel).

You can also review all messages sent by clicking on *Message Log*.

Chapter 4

Sample Lesson Plans and Tutorials

The previous chapters have given an overview of how teachers and administrators are using student cell phones coupled with free or low-cost Internet resources. This chapter focuses on specific lesson plans for using cell phones in classroom learning. These activities couple cell phones and free (or low-cost) web resources to create powerful learning activities. These activities focus on using phone calls, text messages, or cell phone cameras. Most of these features are standard on most cell phones, maximizing student access for participation in the activities. Further, there are a variety of subject areas and grade levels covered in these lessons. Each lesson includes a tutorial on how to use the Web 2.0 resource coupled with the cell phone. Although most lessons are subject specific, keep in mind that these lessons (and the cell phone resources) can be tweaked to fit into any subject area for Grades 6–12.

The lesson plans are separated into three types: phone calling activities, texting activities, and phoning and texting activities. Phone calling lesson plans (Lesson Plans 1–6) focus on using the audio features of the cell phone (making a phone call). In addition, many of these resources have toll-free calling numbers or local area codes so that students who do not have their own cell phones can still use a landline to participate in the activities. The text-messaging lesson plans (Lesson Plans 7–13) focus on using the text message (SMS) features of the cell phone. Although almost every cell phone can send and receive text messages, not every cell phone service plan includes texting, and many that do have limits on free texts. It is vital that students know their cell phone plans so that they do not incur overcharges. All of the following activities can work on a basic phone with SMS texting. The phone calling and texting lesson plan (Lesson Plan 14) allows for the use of both phone calls and text messages.

Lesson Plan 1   *Inspired by Jimbo Lamb*

Connecting Algebra to the Real World

Content Area	Mathematics
Type of Activity	Phone calling
Web 2.0 Resource	Yodio

About Yodio

Yodio (www.yodio.com) is a free web-based application that allows anyone to set up an account and then use a cell phone to call and record a voice message into a private Yodio account. The audio file will automatically be posted in the caller's Yodio account. Then, the caller can log in to Yodio and use the MP3 audio files to create a digital storybook. Yodio allows anyone the ability to upload pictures into the digital storybook editor, where they can drop and drag the audio files and assign them to individual pictures. When finished in the editor, the result is a professional-looking digital storybook. The storybooks can be public or private.

Lesson Description

Students will use their cell phones to record their everyday interactions with algebra. When students encounter an everyday experience outside of school where they recognize that they are using algebra, they will call in to Yodio and record an audio file of what they were doing as well as how it related to algebra. In Yodio, students can add images to create a digital story about their everyday algebra experiences.

Process

1. The teacher goes to http://yodio.com and signs up for a new account.

2. Once the teacher has created an account and logged in, the teacher adds the students' cell phone numbers to the account (so that students can post to the class account). The teacher then clicks on *Add a Phone Number*.

In Class

3. The teacher explains the assignment to the students. Students are expected to program the Yodio phone number into their cell phones. When they encounter an everyday algebra mathematics phenomenon, they call in to

Yodio and describe the situation. They are also encouraged to take a picture of the experience.

Outside Class

4. Students document their everyday algebra experiences by calling in to Yodio and taking pictures.

Back in Class

5. The teacher takes the students to the computer lab (or uses laptop computers) and asks the students to open up the Yodio site.

Yodio account screen with multiple projects

6. At the Yodio site, the students click on *Image*. They can upload any images associated with their Yodio project (it may be something that they recorded such as an image from iPhoto on their own computer or an image from a Creative Commons–appropriate license on the web such as http://behold.cc).

7. Once the images have been added, students click on *Create Yodio*.

8. They then click on *Create a Standard Blank Yodio*.

9. Students can now browse and upload images and drag them to the Yodio Track Window.

10. Next they can click on *Choose Audio* and drag the audio track to the Yodio track window.

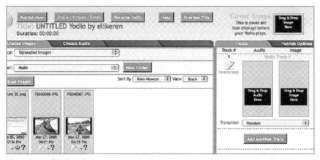

Once media has been uploaded, you can combine and edit it by dragging and dropping

11. When they finish, they click on *Publish Now.*

12. They need to add a title, description, keyword, and so on. Once they finish, their completed story is available online.

13. The Yodio will pop up. Students can also embed their Yodio slide shows into other websites or blogs.

Details for a completed Yodio clip

Extensions

- Students can record their observations or interviews on a field trip via their cell phones. They can take photos via their cell phones to document their learning. When they return to class from the field trip, they can open up Yodio and edit their digital storybooks to reflect what they learned.

- Students can record a new ending to a famous novel for homework via their cell phone. For example, for the book *Animal Farm*, teachers could ask the students to create a new ending by using visual imagery. Students could take pictures of different everyday activities that inspire a new ending to the book, such as a picture of two animals playing (representing the different animals in the book coming together in a peaceful agreement to end their differences). Students can record the audio description that relates the images to the characters in the book and the new ending that they have conjured up. Back in class, they can log in to Yodio and put the digital storybook together.

- To enhance their oral language skills, foreign language students could insert an image in Yodio (or take a photo with their cell phones) and then describe the scene in the foreign language.

Lesson Plan 2

Inspired by Paul Wood

Virtual Debate

Content Area	Social Studies
Type of Activity	Phone calling
Web 2.0 Resource	Google Voice

About Google Voice

Google Voice (http://google.com/voice) is a free application that allows anyone to sign up and receive a free local phone number. Google Voice is a private web-based voicemail system that can couple with any phone to work like traditional voicemail. It can transcribe speech to text for any voicemails. Every voicemail left in your Google Voice account automatically becomes an MP3 file that can be downloaded or used anywhere on the web. In Google Voice online, you can send text messages, make phone calls, and create unique greetings for individuals or specific groups of callers. A teacher can create a group for parents, then select the group "parents" when they want to send out a mass text message or give them a unique greeting. If someone calls you using your Google Voice phone number, you can record the conversation as it happens.

Lesson Description

Students will use their cell phones to record their own debate. Students will call in to the Google Voice number (given to them by their teacher). They will then hear an assignment where the teacher instructs them to give a perspective on a current event that they have been studying.

Process

1. Sign up for a free Google Voice account (http://google.com/voice). Google Voice is available only in the United States at this time.

2. Google Voice provides the teacher with a local phone number. This phone number can be redirected to many different phone options (landlines, cell phones, or direct to voicemail). This allows the teacher to give the students a phone number without having to give the teacher's real cell or landline phone number.

3. The teacher receives an email with a verification link that allows login to the new Google Voice account.

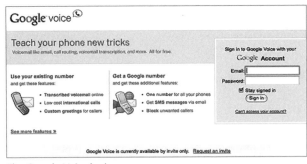

The Google Voice login screen

4. The teacher creates a voicemail greeting in Google Voice with an assignment about current events. The greeting could be: "Do you think that the United States should have a universal health care system with a public option? Please select a viewpoint, provide evidence from reliable resources, and cite those resources."

5. To create the voicemail greeting, the teacher needs to click on Settings, then select the *Voicemail & SMS* tab. When you are ready, click on *Record New*.

The Google Voice Settings screen

6. Name the recording. Google Voice then calls your cell phone (or whichever phone you had selected) when you click on *Connect*. Once the phone rings and you answer it, you will be given directions on how to record the voicemail greeting. When finished, hang up.

7. Make sure the Voicemail Greeting is the new one you created. Select whether you prefer a text message or email when new voicemails arrive. Click on *Save Changes*.

8. Select *Calls*, then click on *Enable "Do Not Disturb."* This keeps your phone from ringing and allows all calls to go directly to voicemail. Click on *Save Changes*.

Choose Enable "Do Not Disturb" to have student voice messages go directly to your phone's voicemail

9. Give the students the phone number and ask them to call in *after* they have read the current-event readings for the night (the readings should focus on current controversial issues in politics such as stem cell research, gun control, or the death penalty). The students should be told that their assignment is to defend one of the current events or take a stance. They don't need to agree with the position they take, but they do need to garner evidence to support the position. They should be prepared to do this before calling in. Students have the option of calling in, listening to the assignment, hanging up, and calling back when they are ready to record.

Outside the Classroom

After reading the current-event articles, students call in (with a cell phone or landline because it is a local phone call), listen to the voicemail greeting assignment, and then give their debate speeches (about 5 minutes). Set up Google Voice so that you receive a text message every time a speech has been posted, so you'll know to go in and listen to the speech (or hear it via their cell phone).

Log back into http://googlevoice.com and see if the students' voicemail debates are all in the Inbox of Google Voice. You can listen to each speech, evaluate the speeches online, and by using the SMS button below each student's speech, text each student back with the evaluation.

Back in Class

You may select one or two speeches from students who did an exemplary job gathering evidence for their chosen side of the debate.

Extensions

- Students who are hearing-impaired can take advantage of the free transcription feature. It allows these students to receive phone calls as transcribed text. In addition, they can take advantage of using SMS texting in Google Voice to respond to group members. A record of all group conversations can be captured in Google Voice.

- Teachers can also take advantage of the live recording feature that allows them to document their conversations (with students and parents) by recording phone calls. Of course, the teacher needs to inform the parent or student on the other end of the line that the conversation will be recorded. If the parent or student declines being recorded, the teacher should document the call by taking notes.

Lesson Plan 3

Live Student Radio Station

Content Area	All
Type of Activity	Phone calling
Web 2.0 Resource	BlogTalkRadio

About BlogTalkRadio

BlogTalkRadio (http://blogtalkradio.com) is a free web-based resource that allows anyone to create their own live Internet radio show. BlogTalkRadio works in a similar fashion to a radio show—you can set up shows and get them started by calling in via cell phone, upload recorded audio, include live call-ins from listeners, conduct a live chat room, and all the shows are automatically archived on the site. BlogTalkRadio also includes an RSS feed and embedding widgets with every show.

Lesson Description

Students will participate in a yearlong weekly live podcast. The topic of the podcast can vary (by subject area), or it can be the student radio station for the whole school. The podcast could also consist of live broadcasting of sporting events.

Process

Inside School

1. Begin the project by discussing cell phone safety, etiquette, appropriate use, and agreed-on rules (see Chapter 5 for more information on digital footprints and safety). With the students watching, create an account in BlogTalkRadio that will become the class radio station. Log in to http://blogtalkradio.com.

2. Click on *Broadcast Now*. When you register, make sure that everyone agrees on a login and password (each student will be using the log in and password as they take turns moderating and hosting the show). Once you register and confirm your email, you will be able to create the Internet radio show.

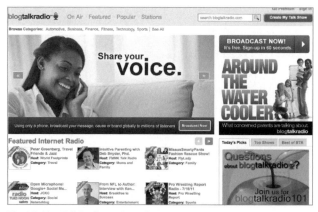

The MyBlogTalkRadio main web page

3. Click on *Create my own free radio show.* Click on *Schedule Your First Show.*

4. Click on *My Account,* then select *Add new episode.* Now you and the students can add the first episode along with a description for the show. They must include keywords and a date/time for the show.

MyBTR > Episodes

Here you can create new segments, view or edit upcoming segments or shows from your archive.
Please note that it could take a minute or two before a scheduled segment can be viewed on the show page.

Add new episode	Upcoming episodes	Archived episodes	Recurring episodes

To create more than one segment, simply click multiple boxes (preferably the same day each week) in the calendar below and they will be scheduled at the same time. You can schedule shows up to 30 days in advance. You can set up a recurring segment that will automatically add the shows for you as necessary.

* = Required

Title	
Description	

2000 characters remaining

IMPORTANT: Descriptions are a very important part of how listeners will find and decide to listen to your content, plus part of how we evaluate episodes to be featured. We recommend that you keep your description brief, while including pertinent details about guests and content. Don't forget to include keywords people might use to search for your content!

Tags or keywords

Please enter all 5 keywords that best describe this episode. Keywords can help organic search results and ultimately drive more traffic to your show. Think about words your target audience might search to find your content. Use words like guest names, topics, and details. Be specific!

The Episode Creation screen

5. After you hit *Submit,* the show is set up under Upcoming Episodes.

Browsing upcoming shows in MyBlogTalkRadio

6. When it is time for the show to begin, the student or students in charge of the show log back into BlogTalkRadio (with the login and password that the teacher set up). Click on *My BlogTalkRadio*, then click on *My Account*. In My Account, click on *Switchboard*. The Switchboard will open and give the information for hosting the show. Students will first call in to the Host Number and follow the audio directions. They will click #2 to host their shows.

7. If there are any cohosts or other participants (such as a guest for the show), they can call in to the Guest Call-In Number. On the Switchboard, the host will be able to let the other callers into the show and open the chat room. When the show is over, it will be archived automatically on the radio site, allowing other people to listen to and download the show.

Extensions

- Students could create their own radio podcasts on curricular topics of their interest (such as a podcast on exotic animals for biology class, or a podcast on future jobs for seniors who are beginning to explore the job market, or a podcast on music appreciation for the instrumental music class).

Lesson Plan 4

Inspired by Katie Titler

Spanish-Speaking Avatar

Content Area   Foreign Language
Type of Activity   Phone calling
Web 2.0 Resource Voki

About Voki

Voki (http://voki.com) is a free web-based application that allows anyone to create their own avatars. An avatar is a web-based cartoon-like depiction of a person's alter ego. Voki allows people to design their own avatars, including the background, and give the avatar a voice. One way to give the avatar a voice is by using a cell phone. Voki can call a cell phone (or a landline if the student does not have a cell phone), or by using a toll-free 1-800 number, you can call in to Voki and give the avatar your own voice!

Lesson Description

Students will create a personal Spanish avatar for their yearlong Spanish course. They will use the avatar to practice oral communication and demonstrate cultural understanding.

Process

1. Before class, set up a class Voki account by going to http://voki.com and clicking on *Login*.

The Voki splash page

2. Reserve the computer lab (or laptops) for the day you are introducing the project. Tell students to bring their cell phones.

In Class

3. Review cell phone etiquette, safety, and class rules around cell phone use before starting the project (see Chapter 5 for these).

4. Ask students to log in to http://voki.com, then ask students to click on *CREATE*, where they will be able to make their own Voki avatar. First they can select a character and adjust and customize its appearance.

5. Next they can give their avatar a voice by calling in with their cell phone (if students do not have cell phones, they can type in the avatar or use their internal computer microphone to record).

Voki's avatar customization page

6. After the students call in their recording, they should click on Save to save the recording. Next, they can add a background.

7. Now, they can click on *Publish* and click on *Sign up*. Students can log in to the account you created for the class using your email and password. (Before beginning this exercise, you should create a special Gmail, Yahoo!, or other free email account so you are not giving out your personal account information.)

8. After students log in, they will be able to view their avatars in Voki and can also email, embed, or send you a link to their avatars.

A completed Voki Avatar

The avatar's background and voice can change according to the teacher's focus. Students can take oral quizzes or practice speaking. Also, they can change the background to include personal pictures, or pictures that represent the oral speeches.

Extensions

- Students could also use their avatars to demonstrate their cultural knowledge by changing the background pictures and character's appearance to be more relevant to the culture they are learning about.

Lesson Plan 5

Audio Blogging in Foreign Languages

Content Area	Foreign Language
Type of Activity	Phone calling
Web 2.0 Resource	ipadio

About ipadio

ipadio (http://ipadio.com) is a free web-based application that enables anyone to record audio from their cell phone directly to the web. One of the bonus features of this application is that it has cross-posting. Cross-posting allows for the ipadio audio feeds to post directly on just about any blog (rather than having to embed each individual feed).

Lesson Description

Students in foreign language class will be able to practice their oral speaking skills by posting audio blogs onto their blog. They will set up an ipadio account that will cross-post directly to their Blogger blog (one can use a variety of social networking resources, not just Blogger). This way, students can call in to ipadio, speak their homework and then within minutes it will post on their blog without the need to embed a link.

Process

The teacher sets up a blog for the class using Blogger (or another social media resource). Next, the teacher guides the students through setting up their ipadio accounts. Here is how.

In Class

1. Students will log in to http://ipadio.com and click on *Sign Me Up*. They will need to put in their phone numbers (and they can put in multiple numbers such as a landline because it is a toll-free number).

2. Once registered, they can set up their phone account. Students should click on *My Profile* and then click on the *Channel Details* tab. When students call in to ipadio, it will ask for the PIN, so they might want to change the PIN to something that they will remember. They should also check *Enable speech-to-text conversion*.

The ipadio splash screen/register page

3. Now they can click on the *Social Media* tab (this is where they will enable the cross-posting to the class blog). Students should scroll down until they reach Blogger. In Blogger they should type in the following email: (name of login) + ipadio @blogger.com.

Configuring ipadio to synch with Blogger

4. Students should click *Update Settings* (to save this). Next the teacher should log in to the class blog on Blogger and in the Settings, click on *Email & mobile*. When prompted, type in "ipadio" to the *Email posting address*. Now, students can record their audio blogs.

   To record and post, students call 1-888-488-3946 and follow the instructions. When they finish and publish, they should hang up. Their audio blog will appear both in their ipadio account and on the class blog!

Extensions

- Students could also create their own podcasts or radio shows with ipadio (and not cross-post to a blog). Visually impaired students could also use ipadio to "speak" where written text is asked for (especially because ipadio has speech-to-text transcription free with every account).

Lesson Plan 6

Student Organizer

Content Area	All
Type of Activity	Phone calling
Web 2.0 Resource	Dial2Do

About Dial2Do

Dial2Do (www.Dial2Do.com) is a low-cost speech-to-text phone application that couples with a wide variety of Web 2.0 applications to allow the student to "speak" a task or "listen" to a webpage. With one phone call to Dial2Do, the student can choose to send a text message, send an email, post to a Google Calendar, post to a blog, translate language, listen to email, listen to a calendar, set reminders, and much more! When the student calls in, Dial2Do will ask, "What would you like to do?" The student should say "text," and the person or group the student wishes to send a text message to, and finally the student records the message. Dial2Do will then transcribe the speech to text and send the text message! The student will also receive an archive of all the messages and posts that were created in a private Dial2Do account (both audio and text versions are available).

Lesson Description

Students will replace their hardcopy student planners with their cell phones and Dial2Do. They will use Dial2Do to remind themselves of assignments and school activities. In addition, they can use Dial2Do to text or email groups for group activities and assignments.

Process

1. Go over cell phone safety and digital footprints before starting the project.

2. Have students log in to http://Dial2Do.com and register to create a Dial2Do account. When students register, they need to include their cell phone number (this will let Dial2Do automatically know who is calling when they call the general number).

Dial2Do's registration page

3. After students register, they can begin to set up their mobile planners. First they may need to confirm their email address and log in. If students want to add another number to their Dial2Do account, they can do this by clicking on *Settings* (students can add multiple numbers to one account).

4. Now, students can click on *Contacts*. Students can add their friends, teachers, family members, and professional contacts, including email addresses and cell phone numbers. After students have added their contacts, they can also create groups (this allows the students to send an email or text message to an entire group of people at once).

Dial2Do's contacts and group settings

5. Once students have set up their contacts, they can click on *Do More*. In Do More, students can add new activities that become available when they call in to Dial2Do. For example, they can add email by clicking on *Add* or send reminders by clicking on *Add*. If there is a class calendar on Google, or a personal calendar, students can add the *Calendar* link (they can easily

make one if they do not have one). Now, if they want to set up a reminder or send an email, they can call in to the Dial2Do number 1-213-325-2615 and say "reminder" or "email" and follow the instructions. After Dial2Do says "That's done," the students can do more.

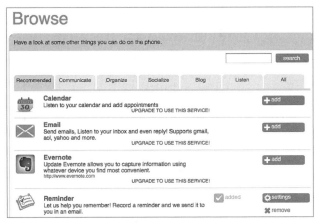

Adding new activities to Dial2Do

When students are finished, all of their activities will be archived under *My Activities* in Dial2Do. (Also, if the student sends an email, it will show up in the email account of the recipient as both an audio file and speech-to-text transcribed file.)

Extensions

- Besides posting speech to text, to calendars, and emails, or reminders students can also listen to them. When they call in to Dial2Do, they say, "Listen to email," or "Listen to calendar," and then they can hear what they have scheduled.

- Students can also post blogs to their blog accounts. Under *Do More*, students can select their type of blog (Blogger, Tumblr, Wordpress, TypePad, etc.). Then, they will be able to call in to Dial2Do and say, "Blogger" and they will be able to post a speech-to-text blog post!

Lesson Plan 7

Inspired by Judy Pederson

Controversies in Science

Content Area Science
Type of Activity Text messaging
Web 2.0 Resource ChaCha

About ChaCha

ChaCha (www.chacha.com) is a free resource that allows anyone to make a phone call (1-800-2chacha) or send a text message with a question (CHACHA) to ChaCha. ChaCha has a person (called a guide) who will receive the question and search for the answer. The guide will return the answer, via text message, within minutes. Although there is no cost for using ChaCha (outside of regular text messaging fees from individual service plans), advertisements are included in the text messages back from ChaCha.

Lesson Description

Students will research a science topic that generates controversy such as global warming, evolution, or the benefits of stem cell research. They will use ChaCha as a starting point for their research by calling or texting some inquiry questions to ChaCha, such as "What are some possible causes of global warming?" or "What are the possible benefits of stem cell research?" Students will present their findings before the end of class.

Process

In Class

1. Give the students a handout with a list of controversial scientific topics that you believe are appropriate to study. Examples might include "Is global warming real?" "Are there guaranteed benefits of stem cell research?" "Should space programs be funded?" "What is the best fuel option for the future?" "Should Pluto be considered a planet?" "Should animal experiments continue?" "Are the benefits of cloning worth the risks?"

2. Ask the students to consider probing questions to start their research.

3. Allow students to text or call ChaCha to get as far as possible in their research. Explain to the students that they will have to come to an educated conclusion as to the main cause of something, the greatest benefit, or the least likely outcome (depending on the question) by using the evidence that they gather from ChaCha. They need to include references in their final papers (make sure they ask for the references from ChaCha!).

Extensions

- Rather than just a 50-minute class period, allow the students to conduct research over a longer period of time.

Lesson Plan 8

Student Business Cards

Content Area	Business/Economics
Type of Activity	Text messaging
Grade Level	High School
Web 2.0 Resource	Contxts

About Contxts

Contxts (www.contxts.com) is a free website that allows anyone to create a mobile business card with a unique keyword. When somebody sends a text to Contxts to request the mobile business card, they will receive all of the pertinent information on their cell phone. In addition, Contxts collects all of the names and numbers of the people who request a user's mobile business card in the user's private account.

Lesson Description

Students will create their own mobile business cards that they can share with potential employers and others for networking purposes.

Process

1. Students go to http://contxts.com and click on *Get It Free!*

2. Students create their accounts and select usernames (which will become their keywords for text messaging, so they should select something related to themselves and that sounds professional). Click on *Submit*.

3. Next, students will click on *Edit Info*.

4. In *Edit*, students add the information they would like to have in their mobile business cards (140 characters or less). This is a great opportunity to talk with students about pertinent information for business cards. Students could even include a link to an online resume or ePortfolio. Students will click on *Submit* when they finish.

5. Students can try out their new business cards (and ask their classmates to do the same) by text messaging their keywords to 50500.

A sample Contxts business card

Outside Class

6. Ask the students to begin to give out their business cards to local business people.

Back in Class

7. Discuss with students their experiences with giving out the business cards and ask if they received any feedback about the content or process.

Extensions

- Each student in a class can create a "business card" as a 140-character flash card, giving it a keyword. As a result, all the students in the class could exchange different flash cards for review. If the cards are saved on the students' phones, then the students can use them anytime for an instant review.

- Students who are struggling with issues of depression, addiction, disease, anxieties, peer pressure, or other afflictions are often fearful to tell an adult. Giving students mobile business cards with help-line information means they can contact the lines at any time without fear of being identified.

- Teachers can create keyword scavenger hunts using Contxts. For example, a teacher can create "clues" by using the 140-character business cards, and as students answer the clues and find the new locations for the scavenger hunt, they text a new keyword and receive a new clue. This would be a fun activity for students learning local history, math students studying geometry, physics students, or even foreign language students. (Students could explore a designated area in the city, or just the school, unraveling clues in other languages.)

- Students could team up with local businesses to create 140-character advertisements. For example, students might create an ad slogan for a local coffee shop, and combine it with a coupon: "Drink a cup of Joe before 8 & Get a rebate ... COUPON CODE: 721u." Students could create posters or a word-of-mouth campaign to try to get people to call in to hear the advertisement and the coupon code.

Lesson Plan 9   *Inspired by Jarrod Robinson*

Homework Help in Math

Content Area   Mathematics
Type of Activity   Text messaging
Web 2.0 Resource   Kaywa

About Kaywa

Kaywa (www.kaywa.com) is a free website that allows anyone to create quick response (QR) codes. QR codes are essentially bar codes for cell phones. Using a QR code reader on your cell phone (which you can download free from Kaywa), you can take a picture of a QR code and immediately receive information on your phone associated with that QR code (it could be text, a picture, a web link, an email address, or even a movie!). At Kaywa, it is very easy to create your own QR code. Once it has been created, you can post it on the Internet, include it in a digital document, or print it off and use it on hard copy.

Lesson Description

The teacher will add QR codes to math homework assignment sheets. The QR codes will contain information such as tutorials, real-world examples, and links on how to help the students solve the math problems. Students will use their cell phones to take pictures of the QR codes on the assignment sheet to get the necessary math help.

Process

1. Create or select the math worksheets for homework. Then, using Kaywa, create the QR codes that provide the students with extra hints and help for solving the math problems on the worksheet. To do this, go to http://qrcode.kaywa.com.

2. Create the QR codes by selecting *Text*. In the *Text* box, add a hint for the first math problem on the page (or a general hint/tip for the whole page of problems). Then, click on *Generate*. The QR code will appear in the box. Right-click and copy it and paste it into a Word document worksheet. Continue to create codes and paste them into the worksheet until there is enough help information on the worksheet. Print off the worksheets for the students.

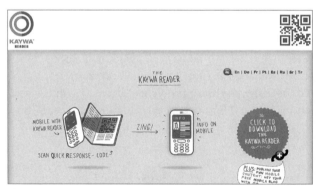

A QR code and its associated text

In Class

3. Help the students download the QR code readers onto their phones and ask all the students to log in to: www.kaywa.com. Have them click on *Kaywa Reader*. Students will be able to download the reader to their phones.

The Kaywa QR code Reader download page

4. Hand out the worksheets and ask the students to take a cell phone picture of one of the QR codes on their worksheet to make sure it works.

Outside Class

5. Students can use the QR codes to help them with their homework.

Extensions

- Students could develop their own QR codes. They could create a website, blog, or image that reflects the content they are studying (such as a website about the history of lighthouses in Michigan or an image of a collage they created to represent metamorphosis), and then generate a QR code for it. Next they could post their QR codes all over the school/community/web where people can read them.

- The teacher could make up QR codes for different topics being studied in a unit. The students could post them all over the community (almost like a treasure hunt), where students would find the clue by using their QR code reader; solve it, revealing the location of the next QR code; and find the next QR code. In the end, by solving the mystery, they learn about the content in the unit.

- Teachers could team up with a local business and the students would develop an advertising campaign for them. Part of the campaign could include use of QR codes.

- Students could create QR codes for their portion of a group project or review (such as defining some concepts). They could generate QR codes so that they could share their reviews with other students.

Lesson Plan 10   *Inspired by Rebekah Randall*

Chemical Elements in Real Life

Content Area   Science (Chemistry)
Type of Activity   Text messaging
Web 2.0 Resource   Cellblock

About Cellblock

Cellblock (http://cellblock.com) is a free web-based service where anyone can send pictures or videos from their cell phone into a public or private slideshow feed. It is incredibly easy to set up and use: A person creates an account and gets a mobile email address to which pictures can be sent from any cell phone! The pictures appear immediately in a slide show and the user may add optional text. There are also some nice privacy settings on Cellblock. A teacher only needs to set up one account for use with all of the student cell phones (thus, no need for student accounts, and the teacher can control editing).

Lesson Description

Students will use their cell phones to take pictures of everyday activities related to the study of chemical elements. They will then use their images in their classroom chemistry studies. This activity will help students put an image to each chemical element.

Process

   1. Go to http://cellblock.com, click on *Sign Up*, and register for an account.

The Cellblock sign-up page

2. Then click on *Start a new cellblock*. Add a new Cellblock Title and information (click on *Security Settings* for privacy options).

3. Write down the "Send pix to" email address (this is what you give to students so that they can send pictures from their phones into the class account).

Starting a new cellblock page

In Class

4. Review mobile safety with the students (see Chapter 5 for details). Introduce the periodic table to the students. Explain that for each chemical element that is studied, the students will be taking pictures from their everyday lives to represent the elements (they could be in compound form as long as the students recognize that there are multiple elements in the object/item they took a picture of—such as water). They will be sending their pictures to Cellblock.

5. Give students the Cellblock mobile email address, and tell them to save the address in their cell phone contacts so that they always have it with them. *Note:* If students do not have cell phones, they can still email pictures with this same address from a computer.

6. Students should take practice pictures in class with their phones and send these to the Cellblock site.

Outside Class

7. Students will take mobile pictures of different examples of the elements in the periodic table in their day-to-day lives. They should send the pictures directly to the Cellblock account along with text about the element that is involved in the everyday object.

Back in Class

8. Open the Cellblock account and discuss all the different materials found that contain each element. You can take the assignment further by asking students to investigate where these elements are found and how they become the everyday objects that were photographed.

Extensions

- Students could post mobile images to create a storybook. If students had their own Cellblock accounts, they could each have their own storybook (and this would be created in the moment—in real time).

- This would be a fun way to create a storyboard for a video project. Students could text in images and text describing the different scenes.

- With parents' permission, the school could create a Cellblock image feed of school activities and events. Parents could follow and stay up-to-date as well as being able to participate by adding their own comments.

- Research report: Twitter style. Students could put together their own inquiry-based image project to research a topic, provide evidence, and reach a conclusion. For example, they could use images to describe what they believe to be the greatest cause of the current economic crisis, or evidence of whether or not global warming is a real phenomenon. Images can be a powerful way to present a well-thought-out research study.

Lesson Plan 11   *Inspired by Larry Liu*

A Novel Connection

Content Area   English
Type of Activity   Text messaging
Web 2.0 Resource   Mobile Facebook

About Mobile Facebook

Mobile Facebook (www.facebook.com). The social networking site Facebook has an option for users to send images, text, or video directly from their cell phones into a Facebook account.

Lesson Description

Students reading a class novel will take pictures from their everyday lives that they believe relate to the characters, settings, plot, and themes in the novel. For example, if the students are reading *The Great Gatsby*, they could take pictures of a mansion in the community to represent Gatsby's home. They will post them to the class Facebook page via their cell phones.

Process

In Class

1. Begin the lesson by going over the norms of social networking, creating appropriate profiles, postings, and the permanence of social networking. Include the following ideas:

   - Don't assume anything you send or post is going to remain private.

   - There is no changing your mind in cyberspace—anything you send or post will never truly go away.

   - Don't give in to the pressure to do something that makes you uncomfortable, even in cyberspace.

   - Consider the recipient's reaction.

   - Nothing is truly anonymous.

In addition, you should teach students about how the Internet and social networking sites are archived by using an example such as The WayBack Machine (www.archive.org). Show students the movie *Digital Dossier* (www.youtube.com/watch?v=79IYZVYIVLA) to reinforce the public nature of digital records. Students could take the Digital Footprint quiz (http://dsc.discovery.com/convergence/koppel/interactive/interactive.html).

2. Develop a social contract with students about what is and is not appropriate to post on their Facebook sites.

3. With the students, set up a Facebook Profile (or Fan Page). Go over signing up and changing your privacy settings. Log in to http://facebook.com and sign up. Make sure to click on the *skip* link when setting up the profile (demonstrating to students that they don't have to include everything about themselves or add friends right away).

4. Continue to skip until you get to the profile picture (here is the place to talk with students about having an appropriate profile picture because this is the first image that future employers and relations will see). Once you've added an appropriate profile picture, click on the page name in the upper right-hand corner.

Facebook's profile picture page

5. With the basic class page showing, go over the privacy settings with the students. Click on *Settings*, then *Privacy Settings*.

6. In *Privacy Settings*, click on each option and talk with students about making them as restricted as possible (by selecting *Only Friends* or *Only You*). When finished, it is time to set up the cell phone posting options for the students.

Facebook's privacy settings page

7. Click on *Your Name—My Account*, then select the *Mobile* tab on the My Account page. You'll see three options for mobile connections. Chose *Upload via Email* (it is the easiest to manage for this exercise).

More Facebook Mobile Products

Facebook Text Messages
- Update your Status and Message friends using text messages.
- Receive SMS texts with Status Updates, Messages and Wall Posts as they happen.

Sign Up for Facebook Text Messages

Upload via Email
Use a personalized upload email to post status updates or send photos and videos straight to your profile. Your personal email is:

baalim878peaked@m.facebook.com

Send my upload email to me now

Find out more

Facebook for your phone
Download rich, interactive applications built for your phone. Available for:

iPhone	Nokia
Palm	Android
Sony Ericsson	Windows Phone
INQ	Sidekick
Blackberry	

Facebook's Mobile Products page

8. Give students the mobile email address to the class site (ask them to add it as a new contact on their phones). Go over mobile posting rules, making sure the students understand that they need to ask permission before posting images of other people to the Facebook account. Have them try a practice post by sending a video, text, or picture to the site from their cell phones.

9. Ask the students to add the new class profile as a "friend" (if they can't do this in school, they can do it at home). Ask students to go home and clean up their Facebook profiles and remind them that teachers are obligated to report anything inappropriate that they see on their students' profiles! (The key word is "ask"; you cannot force the students to change, but let them know that you will be casually monitoring—and their future employers may be as well.)

10. Let students know that for each chapter they read, they will be taking pictures of different everyday occurrences that they think are related to the novel. Students should take pictures that they believe represent the setting, the characters, and different parts of the storyline. In addition, you should ask the students to text (or say in the mobile videos) why they believe these images represent the novel.

Outside Class

11. Each student will take pictures or videos with their cell phone and send them to the class Facebook page (via the Facebook email address).

Back in Class

12. Open the Facebook page each day and select a few images or videos to be the focal point for the class discussion.

Extensions

- Because students are "friends" with the class Facebook page, they can comment and discuss the images and videos for homework before coming to class.

- You can also use the site to communicate with students (and parents who are on Facebook) for office hours, organization, homework help, class signups, and assignments.

Hints for Students Using Facebook

- Take control of your photos. Personal and professional lives are becoming one, largely due to Facebook. Go through what you have on your social network and "untag" yourself in photos that an employer might find inappropriate.

- Set privacy settings. You have less reason to worry if employers can't access your digital life.

- Post photos that promote you as a professional. If you have photos from volunteering, studying abroad, working a job, giving a presentation, or any other semiprofessional event, post them. They go a long way to help counteract other photos that might negatively impact your image.

- Put up a "clean" profile photo of yourself. Even if you got a lot of compliments on your wild Halloween costume, a profile picture that isn't associated with raucous partying means a lot to people in hiring positions.

- Stay active online. By commenting on blogs and forums, updating your profiles, and even creating your own site, you can become much more visible and credible online. This gives the people who search for you a much more comprehensive picture of who you are, and allows you to highlight the good and bury the bad.

- Be mindful of who you accept as a "friend." Poor choices could reflect badly on you as a professional. Make sure to monitor your friends' comments on your sites as well.

Lesson Plan 12

Social Studies Scavenger Hunt

Content Area	Social Studies (Local History)
Type of Activity	Text messaging
Web 2.0 Resource	SCVNGR

About SCVNGR

SCVNGR (http://scvngr.com) is an online resource that allows anyone to participate in (or create their own) mobile scavenger hunts. People can participate in the hunts with basic text messaging—no GPS or smartphone required. It is very easy to create SMS scavenger hunts. SCVNGR uses a fill-in-the-blank type template system to set up a hunt. Once it is set up, students can start the game themselves. Alternatively, you can start the game for all the students by sending a mass text message. The hunt can be anywhere: in a museum, around the city, in the school, at any location, or even in a book. The clues can be mixed differently for each student or group of students so that they do not arrive in the same place at the same time. The hunt can also be timed. When you finish creating a scavenger hunt, you'll receive a downloadable handout for the students, with easy instructions on how to participate in the hunt. Also, the students can include pictures in the hunt and grade the pictures via the SCVNGR website.

Lesson Description

For homework, students will work in groups to complete a mobile scavenger hunt about local history. The students will travel on foot (or by car, depending on how spread out the city is) to find clues and complete challenges at the clue locations. All of the data from the scavenger hunt will be compiled in the teacher's SCVNGR account on the web. This activity should take place over a long weekend or on a school break (such as spring or winter break) to give students enough time to complete their scavenger hunts.

Process

1. Before class, go to http://scvngr.com. Create an account by clicking on *Log In*, then *Register*. When done, log in to your new account and click on *Create a Mission*. Watch the SCVNGR Mission Builder Help Video.

Welcome, Beth

» **Missions You've Built**   Create a Mission

Mission Title
      You have yet to build a mission, let's change that.

» **Quick Stats**

Missions Played   1
Missions Built   0
Total Points   3
   More Stats!

» **Missions You've Played**   Browse Missions

Mission Title   Points
aa22 – Ann Arbor Scav Hunt   3

» **Options**

  Browse Missions
  Create a Mission
  My Photos
  Account Settings

The SCVNGR startup screen

2. Select *Builder* and click on *Trek*. Click *Select Place* and find your city. Fill in the basic information about the trek. r mission—try to keep it between 60 minutes and 90 minutes). Click on *Save & Continue* once again.

Mission Keyword:

          XPLR233   Request Custom Keyword

Mission Title:

    Local History

Max 25 characters, 12 remaining

Where is this mission based?   Enter Nearest City

    Enter Your CITY

Is this a timed mission?   ○ Yes   ● No

Roughly how long do you think the game might take in minutes? Enter Number of Minutes   60 minutes

Please give a verbal description of how long the game might take? Enter Number of Minutes   half a day

                Save & Continue

Creating a SCVNGR mission

3. Fill in a start message. Tell the students where to begin their hunt (a local location). In addition, you should fill out the end-of-game message, telling students what the follow-up will be to the hunt (for example, you could ask them to reflect on the hunt for the next class).

4. Next, select whether you want the students to start the hunt when they get to the location, or if you would like the hunt to automatically start when the students register. You might prefer the Auto Start (just make sure to tell students that the hunt will begin as soon as they text in the keyword). Click on *Save & Continue*.

5. You will be asked to add the clues for the hunt. Complete all the information on the clue page (again, you decide many of the options such as whether you want students to send in pictures of the local historical landmarks and artifacts or if this is to be a timed hunt). Once you've completed the first clue, it will appear in the Review Clues box. You can continue adding clues, but it's best to limit clues to no more than five.

The Clue Generation page

6. Click on *Description* and add a short description of the hunt. Click on *Save & Continue*, then click on *Complete*. Click on *Demoing* (this will make the hunt active). Click on *Review*, where you will be able to download the player instruction cards. These instruction cards tell the students how to play the game (via text message or smartphone). Print out a copy for each group of students.

7. Click back on *Complete*. Under *Demoing*, you will be given codes for playing with basic text message, smartphones, or iPhone and Android apps.

A SCVNGR player instruction card

In Class

8. Explain the project to the students. They will be working in groups of three, traveling around the city or local community (by foot or car). Explain that the hunt should take about 60–90 minutes total, and the results will automatically appear in the teacher's SCVNGR account. Tell them they will be discussing the hunt during their next class meeting.

9. Assign student groups so at least one of the group members has a cell phone that they can use for the hunt. Hand out an instruction sheet to each student. Explain that the hunt will begin when they text in the keyword to the SCVNGR number (all this information is on the instruction handout).

Outside Class

10. Student groups go on their hunts.

Back in Class

11. Open up the SCVNGR site, log in, and click on *My Account*, then click on *View* (next to the mission). Now the whole class will be able to see the Leaderboard and the pictures that were sent from their hunts.

Extensions

- When students finish a test or quiz, there is usually downtime for some of them. They could participate in or create their own mobile scavenger hunt (for example, in an English class students could answer clues about the upcoming novel, or in a science class they could try to answer clues about the upcoming science unit while in their seats waiting for the other students to finish).

- Students could research local history or science phenomena and then create a scavenger hunt for their classmates.

Lesson Plan 13

Inspired by Allison Riccardi

Summarizing Literature

Content Area	English
Type of Activity	Text messaging
Web 2.0 Resource	Wiffiti

About Wiffiti

Wiffiti (http://wiffiti.com) is a free web-based interactive screen that enables anyone with text messaging to send a text message to the board. The message can be anonymous, or accounts can be created to identify who is sending the messages. Wiffiti allows multiple views of the messages (linear and nonlinear) as well as archiving. In addition, if you don't have a cell phone, you can post a message via the web. Wiffiti also integrates Twitter tweets.

Lesson Description

English students will text their 140-character summaries of the homework reading from their class novel to an interactive web screen. This activity could be done during class or for homework.

Process

1. Set up a free Wiffiti screen by going to http://wiffiti.com and clicking on *Sign Up*. Once you've created an account, click on *Make a Screen*, where you can select the options to have on your screen, and then click *Publish Screen*.

The screen options settings in Wiffiti

2. Now the screen is done and ready for students to send messages. Pay attention to the keywords given to the screen at the bottom (these are the numbers that students will need to text in their summaries).

In Class

3. Give the students the number to send a text message to (87884) and the code to put in their message (@wif17118 + summary). Next explain the assignment, asking students to send a 140-character summary of what happened in the homework reading for the night.

Outside Class

4. Students will read their assigned novel and send in their text message summaries to the Wiffiti site.

```
┌──────────────────────────────────────────────────┐
│  ┌──────────────────────────────────────────────┐ │
│  │                                              │ │
│  └──────────────────────────────────────────────┘ │
│  upload an image                ( Post Your Message ) │
│                                                    │
│         Text @wif17118 + your message to 87884     │
└──────────────────────────────────────────────────┘
```

The bottom of a Wiffiti screen, showing the numbers needed to post to the screen

Back in Class

5. Open up the Wiffiti board and go over the summaries, asking students to identify why certain points were focused on in the summaries.

Extensions

• Students could take on different character roles and text from those particular perspectives. Perhaps they could post entries "in the voice" of their book's author. They could text questions they have from the homework reading. The students could translate older English literature such as scenes from Shakespeare into modern chatspeak to show their comprehension of the complex dialogue.

Lesson Plan 14

Everyday Language Instruction

Content Area Foreign Language—Spanish
Type of Activity Phone calling and text messaging
Web 2.0 Resource Tumblr

About Tumblr

Tumblr (www.tumblr.com) is a free blogging resource that lets you post text, photos, quotes, links, music, and videos to a personal website from your browser, phone, desktop, email, or wherever you happen to be. There are no advertisements on Tumblr. Tumblr gives a voicemail number and email address, which can be used on just about any cell phone. The voicemail number can be used to record audio via cell phone that instantly appears in your personal Tumblr webpage as a downloadable MP3 file. In addition, the email address in Tumblr can be used to send pictures or videos from a cell phone into the Tumblr log. This allows just about anyone with a cell phone to collect data that is audio-, video-, or image-based and send it directly to the Tumblr web account.

Lesson Description

When students are participating in their everyday lives outside of school, they think of words or phrases they would like to say in another language. They call in to Tumblr and first say the sentence or question in English and then repeat the sentence or question in the foreign language. Next, they describe how knowing how to communicate this idea is important to being able to acclimate to another culture. Finally, they take a picture or video to capture the moment and send the picture or video to Tumblr via email. This could be a yearlong project where the students are creating their own Tumblr world language reporting blog.

Process

1. Begin by discussing cell phone safety, etiquette, appropriate use, and agreed-on rules (see Chapter 5 for this information). Each student will go to the Tumblr website (www.tumblr.com) and click on *Sign Up* for their own blog.

Tumblr sign-up screen

2. Add an administrative password. (This should be different from the previous password. Only you should know this password, so you have complete control over the site and files on the site.) Once the blog has been created, each student will set up their cell phone to connect with Tumblr by clicking on *Goodies*.

The Tumblr dashboard

3. In Goodies, the students should scroll down to the bottom and get the email address (so they can send pictures, text, and video to their blog) and add the email address to the contacts in their cell phones. In addition, they should click on *Configure* to add their cell phone number to their blog accounts. They should also add the Tumblr phone number to the contacts in their phones.

Post by Email

Email or text message posts to:

reset this address

Post text, photos, MP3s, or videos directly from your email or mobile phone.
Learn more about email publishing.

Call in audio

Create an Audio post from your phone! Just tell us what number to expect the call from.

1-866-584-6757

Configure

Configure Tumblr account to add cell phone number

4. Explain the assignment: Students should find a moment in their everyday lives when they are asking for something or having a conversation that would also be something useful to know how to say in a foreign language. Students should figure out how to say it in Spanish (allow them to call ChaCha or Google 411 to get some tips). Next, call in to the Tumblr voicemail number (1-866-584-6757). Students should say their names first (so you know who has completed the assignment). Ask students to say the statement or question in English and then in Spanish. They should also record why they think it is relevant in both languages and cultures. Finally, ask the students to take a picture of the moment and send it to the blog via the email address.

Back in Class

5. Students can open their Tumblr blogs (or the teacher can do this by projecting their computer), listen to the audio files, and look over the image or video associated with the audio. Discuss the significance of each statement or question, and teach how variations of these statements can be said in the Spanish language.

Extensions

- Students could find someone else who speaks fairly fluent Spanish, explain the project, and "try out" the statements and questions. The student and the other person can have a conversation about it and record the conversation on Tumblr. This will also help them self-test for accuracy in the oral language.

- Students can document a local biography or local science experiment by going to the "real" locations of the topic (such as visiting a local pond where waste is being dumped or interviewing and taking pictures of people who lived through a great historical event). The students can immediately send this data from their cell phones to a Tumblr site, where they can then use the information in class to put together a digital presentation or blog with their "real world" evidence.

- Distance learning projects are easy with the aid of Tumblr. For example, students in a foreign language class can do an e-pals exchange with students in a Spanish-speaking country. They can share video, image, or audio feeds of similar cultural topics (such as "a typical American breakfast" or "a typical school day"), and they can use the blog with their e-pal to communicate experiences back and forth.

Chapter 5

Getting Started

The previous chapters discussed lesson ideas and how teachers and/or administrators are using cell phones every day in schools. This chapter focuses on the planning and preparation process that is necessary in order to start using student cell phones inside and outside of school for instruction. Although it is tempting for some teachers to ask students to take out their cell phones and do a quick text message or phone calling activity without any preparation, it is imperative to be proactive with mindful planning before using student cell phones in any learning activity. Teachers who have used student cell phones advocate extensive preparation before using cell phones in educational settings. Such preparation alleviates potential pitfalls such as inappropriate use of cell phones or incomplete access to cell phones. This chapter guides you through the foundational steps to successfully begin using student cell phones in school learning.

Change Policy

Currently, 70% of schools in the United States have policies that ban student cell phones from the school campus (Common Sense Media, 2009). Although many teachers say this is why they don't use cell phones in learning, these policies are not law. There are no federal or state laws that ban or restrict using student cell phones on a school campus. Rather, the policies are created by individual school districts (sometimes each building in a district has its own policies). The good news is that often individual school policies can be changed or modified easily. You can approach administrators and ask for permission to use your students' cell phones in learning. Of course, you should come armed with a specific proposal and research to support your viewpoint. Following are some pertinent data supporting cell phone use that can help you inform your school administration.

Multiple Access Points

A growing number of people in society use cell phones. As of 2007, 82% of U.S. citizens had cell phones (CTIA—The Wireless Association, 2007). At the secondary level, 98% of students in Grades 9–12 had their own cell phones (Speak Up, 2009). About 44% of students in Grades 3–5 have their own cell phone (Speak Up, 2009). In addition, 27% of K–2 students own cell phones! These numbers are increasing as the younger generation grows up and continues to engage with everyday digital tools. Students' cell phones are ever-present in their lives. Using their cell phones is one way to give students access outside of school to the educational technology resources applied during the school day.

In addition, the ubiquity of cell phones can provide students with a readily available access point for important school information, lessons, and activities. Most schools have a website, and some teachers have webpages—but if students or parents do not have Internet access at home, they may not be able to access vital information or opportunities for learning, participation, and growth. Cell phone resources such as text messaging alerts, voicemail, websites, Twitter, Facebook, and more are readily available, often without cost, on cell phones. By including cell phone options for students and parents, at virtually no cost the school can enhance opportunities for them to participate in the educational process.

Cultural Capital

Not only do students have access to new digital technologies, but the skills they are developing are fast becoming vital in society. Digital skills, such as using the Internet to collaborate, text messaging, chatting, video game playing, and creating cell phone webpages, are future skill requirements for the workforce. For example, the Metiri Group recently reported, "Just twenty years ago, cell phones, laptops, pagers, and fax machines were in the realm of scientists and science fiction. Today, those technologies and the Internet have gained widespread public acceptance and use. It is clear that, in today's Digital Age, students must be technologically literate to live, learn, and work successfully." (Lemke, Coughlin, Thadani, & Martin, 2007). Not only are cell phones becoming ubiquitous in everyday life, they are fast becoming necessary tools for engaging in social and business environments.

Students need to learn the tools and practices that have cultural capital in their communities (Moje & Sutherland, 2003). Digital technology literacy skills and knowledge will be an important form of cultural capital for students, for both democratic citizenship in society and for acquiring jobs in the 21st-century work-force (Lemke et al., 2007; "Transition Brief," 2008).

Fundamental Shift in Citizenship Practices

According to a study conducted by the Pew Internet and American Life Project, concerning the 2008 U.S. presidential election (Smith, 2009), 55% of adults in the United States went online to take part in the political process by gathering news and information, or participating in discussions. The number of adults participating in the political process online has almost doubled in the years since 2004, when only 29% of the adult population went online to participate politically. Over the past five years, the Internet surpassed magazines and radio as a principal source of political information and news for American citizens. In addition, the Pew study found that the younger the population, the more likely they were to rely on the Internet as their primary source of news. During the 2008 campaign, 49% of younger voters (ages 18–24) shared information via text message about the campaigns, and 22% of all cell phone users who voted for Obama (young and old) shared and received campaign information via their cell phones. One in five Internet users posted political commentary online in one or more of the following places: a blog, a social networking site, a discussion board, or a website. Seventy-four percent of all 18- to 24-year-olds were politically active on the Internet during the 2008 campaign. Twenty-six percent of all online voters used the Internet to help them navigate the voting-day process, such as obtaining absentee ballots or learning about their polling places. Although many voters shared their experiences from the polling places on election day, young voters (under the age of 30) were more likely to share experiences via text message, phone call, or a blog post. The shift in U.S. society from print and analog media to digital media is now being reflected in participation in the democratic process.

Fundamental Shift in the Workforce

According to the Partnership for 21st Century Skills ("Transition Brief," 2008), there has been a fundamental shift over the past century in the American economy, workforce, and business that is ultimately reshaping the workplace. More than 80% of new jobs are found in the information service sector, compared to years ago when the majority of jobs were found in the manufacturing sector. Technology has played a large role in these changes. Technological changes are displacing low-skilled workers and making room for workers with skills such as invention, creativity, openness, communication, and global understanding. Many of these skills involve the use of digital technologies. These changes are driving new demands for different types of skills in workers. Employers are calling for schools to integrate new skills into education. Current employers lament that American students are "woefully ill-prepared for the demands of today's (and tomorrow's) workforce" and cite 21st-century skills as "very important" to success in the workplace (Casner-Lotto, Barrington, & Wright, 2006).

Although 81% of future employers ranked information technology skills as "very important" to students' future success, of all the core subject areas only English communication and language were ranked equally or more important. Employers appear to prefer that their workers have more applied skills, as well as solid knowledge in core subject areas: mathematics, science, foreign languages, government/economics, humanities/art, and history/geography. In the report, J. Willard Marriot, Jr., Chairman and CEO of Marriot International, Inc., states:

> To succeed in today's workplace, young people need more than basic reading and math skills. They need substantial content knowledge and information technology skills; advanced thinking skills, flexibility to adapt to change; and interpersonal skills to succeed in multicultural, cross-functional teams. (p. 24)

In addition to future employers, the American voting public is also calling for these same changes in education. In a study conducted by the Partnership for 21st Century Skills (2007), 99% of American voters polled believed that teaching students a wide range of 21st-century skills including computer technology, communication, and media literacy was vital to America's future economic success. In the same study, 80% of voters claimed that the required technical skills students need to be successful in the professional world are vastly different than the required skills of 20 years ago; 42% of voters ranked new media literacy as one of the top skills students needed to be competitive in the workforce; and only 6% of the voters gave schools a high ranking on their ability to teach new media literacies effectively. Similarly, 42% of voters think that other developed countries are doing a better job educating their students in 21st-century skills. These studies point to growing concerns from the American public that students are in serious need of new literacy skills.

Cell Phone Safety and Ethics

Another reason educators are well advised to include student cell phones in their teaching practices is that most students are not aware of digital ethics or safety. If students are expected to integrate 21st-century digital technologies in their future jobs, they also will need to understand and practice ethical and safe practices in using these resources. Unfortunately, often students are unaware of and indifferent to the consequences of their uses of technology (Rainie, 2006). A recent study conducted by Common Sense Media (2009) found that more than 26% of teenagers admitted to using their cell phones to store information to look at during a test or a quiz, 25% have text messaged their friends about answers during a test or quiz, 20% have searched the Internet via their cell phone during a test or quiz, and 17% have taken pictures of a test or quiz with the cell phone to send the images to their friends.

The study further reported that many students do not consider these offenses serious forms of cheating, or even cheating at all. Some students said they were not cheating, but "helping out a friend," when they sent text message answers to their friends or took cell phone photos of tests and sent those along as well. Even more troubling, most of these students are using their cell phones for these activities in schools where the devices are completely banned from campus. In addition, 15% of teenagers have risqué photos of themselves or their friends on their cell phones (Lenhart, 2009). In addition, teenagers feel pressure to share and participate in sexting messages. In a study by Pew (Lenhart, 2009), a high school student wrote, "When I was about 14–15 years old, I received/sent these types of pictures. Boys usually ask for them or start that type of conversation. My boyfriend, or someone I really liked asked for them. And I felt like if I didn't do it, they wouldn't continue to talk to me. At the time, it was no big deal. But now looking back it was definitely inappropriate and over the line." Although students think these messages are fun and private communication between themselves and friends or relations, in some cases when they have been caught exchanging this "sexting" communication, they have been brought up on criminal charges of child pornography.

These statistics indicate a need to teach students about digital appropriateness and safety. Yet less than 5% of educators, in one survey, said that digital safety is included in the state curriculum that they use and less than 3% of those educators said that their state curriculum included information on how to teach students social networking and Internet chat room safety (Hancock, Randall, & Simpson, 2009). In this same study, 60% of teachers admitted that they do not know how or if their schools teach students about cyber bullying, identity theft, or other online safety issues, and 79% said they did not feel prepared to teach students about online digital safety (Hancock et al., 2009). These concerns and the statistics that warrant them demonstrate not only a need for schools to begin educating students about the safe and appropriate use of computers and cell phones, but more importantly a need for teacher educators to better prepare teachers to educate their students on issues of digital media safety. If an important role of the educator is to prepare students for participation in citizenship and the workforce, then educating students about the benefits, responsibilities, and dangers of everyday technology through their uses in school could be one way to meet those challenges.

History of Banning Social Technologies

One of the greatest challenges to technology integration are schools themselves. Historically, many teachers and administrators have been opposed to technical change, even as society has made dramatic technical changes around them. One example is the slate. In 1909, long after paper was easy to obtain and used often in everyday society, most schools still used slates. One reason was a belief that paper could be a health risk to students. Dr. Peter Fraser, late medical officer for Carnarvonshire, England, stated:

> The fact that the writing slate is non-absorbent and consequently can be easily cleansed and disinfected is a great advantage in numerous instances when it is necessary to disinfect schoolrooms and their contents after infectious material has obtained access to the school. On the other hand, paper which has been infected in any way, possibly while in process of manufacture or while being distributed or used, cannot be efficiently disinfected. Paper has to my knowledge been the means of conveying dangerous infection to others. (Slate, n.d.)

Although society had converted to paper almost fifty years prior, schools still insisted on using slates. One reason for schools' resistance to technological change may be that using traditional tools is how the teachers themselves learned, and that was the only vision of learning they knew. Virginia Richardson (1996) found that the kinds of technical tools teachers used when they were students were often the technical tools that they used in their own classroom teaching, no matter how the state of the art might have changed. Although the example of the slates occurred at the turn of the 20th century, concern over integrating popular everyday technology tools into school learning is still an issue well into the 21st century. For example, despite the fact that the Internet, email, and library databases had been publicly available for more than a decade, in 1999 Michael Mowe wrote in the *Montgomery County Herald*:

> The Internet is not a great tool for teaching.… People think that children can think of any topic and pull up a wealth of information on it, but that is not the case. The information in the library is what people seem to expect, but nobody has the time to transcribe entire libraries onto computers. There is nothing on the Internet that is incredibly beneficial to education.

Global Mobile

In many places around the world, cell phones are widely used as learning tools. For example, in Asia, East Asia, and Africa, students can take entire courses via cell phone (including dance and art); write and read novels via mobile devices; use text messaging for homework, quizzes, and communicating with their instructors; learn to become a teacher through mobile devices; use text messaging to support teacher training; and use cell phones as a tool for their exams (Motlik, 2008).

Research Says Cell Phones Can Improve Student Learning

Utilizing everyday technologies in the classroom requires altering current bans; therefore, a strong argument that the benefits outweigh the dangers is necessary. One thread of that argument promotes the contribution that everyday technology will make to students' learning of their subject matter. The discussion in Chapter 1, of research involving situated cognition, pointed out that students learn better when their educational activities are situated in authentic real-world environments using familiar, authentic tools (Brown, Collins, & Duguid, 1989). Further, cognitive growth is fostered by building on existing knowledge (Lee, 2003; Bransford, Brown, & Cocking, 1999). Seymour Papert, a cognitive theorist who developed the LOGO programming language, states that when students enter new learning situations, they may already have the skills for learning something new, but they may not have the knowledge of how to use their prior skills to learn in new ways. They need help in understanding how their prior knowledge can be reconceptualized. Papert says, "Some of the most crucial steps in mental growth are based not simply on acquiring new skills, but on acquiring new administrative ways to use what one already knows" (Minsky, 1988, p. 102). Practically speaking, when students are allowed to create their own learning environments using their prior knowledge, they retain and acquire more knowledge than they would in nonauthentic learning environments (Papert, 1980). Classroom activities are more engaging and enriching when students are supported in making connections between a new task and their prior knowledge. It follows from this understanding that schools could leverage students' own technological knowledge if the tools used in school are the same as those tools and practices that students are already comfortable with in their day-to-day lives.

There have been a few recent studies that identify cell phone use with positive student improvement. The British Academy at Coventry University (2005) found that text messaging can lead to positive literacy growth. In a recent 2010 study, Coventry University found that the proportions of textspeak that children used in their sentence translations was positively linked to verbal reasoning: The more textspeak children used, the higher their test scores. This study claimed that students can develop phonological awareness through text messaging, which in turn helps their ability to spell correctly. A report from the University of Cape Town (Ng'ambi, 2006) found that the anonymity of text messaging lead to greater participation in learning environments and thus greater knowledge growth. Plymouth University (Reid & Reid, 2004) found that text messaging helped shy teenagers communicate their ideas and feelings better.

Survey Students

Once you receive approval from the administration to use student cell phones in your classroom, you need to learn about the mobile technologies and interests of your students. Figure 5.1 shows an example of a survey that was given to students to inquire about their own cell phone capabilities, plans, and interests in using their cell phones.

Figure 5.1 Example of student survey

Mobile Student Survey

Please give them to your students to gather information about their mobile phone knowledge, skills, and plans

Do you have your own cell phone?
○ Yes
○ No
○ No-but I can use my parents anytime

If you have a cell phone, can you send and receive a text message?
○ Yes, I have unlimited texting
○ Yes, but I have limited texting
○ No
○ Other: _____

If you have a cell phone, can you send and receive a picture?
○ Yes, it is part of my unlimited SMS texting plan
○ Yes, but I have to pay extra to do it
○ Yes, I have a limited plan
○ No
○ I can send but not receive
○ I can receive but not send
○ Other: _____

If you have a cell phone, can you send and receive a video?
○ Yes, it is part of my unlimited plan
○ Yes, but I have to pay extra to do it
○ Yes, I have a limited plan
○ No
○ I can send but not receive
○ I can receive but not send
○ Other: _____

If you have a cell phone and you can take videos, how much time do you get per video recording?
○ 30 seconds or less
○ 30seconds to 1 minute
○ 1-2 minutes
○ 2-3 minutes
○ 3-5 minutes
○ 5-10 minutes
○ 10+ minutes

Figure 5.1, *Continued*

Do you have access to mobile Internet on your cell phone?
- ○ Yes and I don't pay extra to use it
- ○ Yes, but I have to pay extra to use it
- ○ No

Do you have GPS or Bluetooth on your phone?
- ○ Yes, and I don't have to pay extra to use it
- ○ Yes, but I have to pay extra to use it
- ○ No
- ○ Other: _____

Do you have MMS messaging?
- ○ Yes, and I don't have to pay extra to use it
- ○ Yes, but I have to pay extra to use it
- ○ No
- ○ Other: _____

Do you believe that the activities you do with your cell phone are private? (eg..texting, taking pictures, phone calls...etc)
- ○ Yes, all of them are private
- ○ Some of them are private
- ○ None of them are private
- ○ Not sure

Please check all the following that you would define as "cheating" with your cell phone
- ☐ Taking a picture of an exam and sending it to a friend
- ☐ sending a friend a question from the exam
- ☐ Using the Internet on your cell phone to look up an answer on an exam
- ☐ Using your cell phone to contact others for help on an exam (during the exam)
- ☐ Texting some hints and tips to a friend about the exam
- ☐ Other: _____

Please check all the following that you would define as "inappropriate use" of a cell phone
- ☐ texting during class
- ☐ answering the phone during class
- ☐ answering the phone at the dinner table
- ☐ texting at the dinner table
- ☐ sending inappropriate pictures of a friend to another friend
- ☐ sending inappropriate pictures of yourself to a friend
- ☐ sending videos of your teacher teaching withour their knowledge
- ☐ texting while driving
- ☐ talking on the phone while driving
- ☐ using a cell phone for your homework assignment (to gather data)
- ☐ Other: _____

Figure 5.1, *Continued*

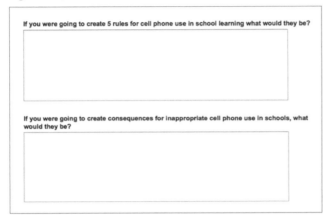

Ideally, this is a survey that students and their parents or guardians should complete together. From this survey you can learn which features are most prevalent on their cell phones. In addition, you will be able to help students understand what they can and cannot do on their cell phones as well as what costs extra (such as accessing the Internet on some phones). You can then begin to consider which features are most accessible on cell phones—for example, 80% of students may have unlimited text messaging while only 40% of students have the ability to view movies on their cell phones. Therefore, you can begin to plan lessons based on the most prevalent features. You can also consider how to group or pair up students who do not have cell phones so those students will participate in lessons and activities without fear of ridicule or embarrassment. This survey may be a helpful conversation piece for parents as well. Parents can use the survey to discuss their own cell phone rules, plans, and expectations with their children.

Cell Phone Safety and Appropriate Use

Before beginning lesson planning (see Chapter 4 for lesson ideas), you must discuss safety and appropriate use of cell phones with the students. Here are three points that are important to any discussion about mobile safety and use.

Mobile activities are part of your digital footprint. Students need to understand that their digital footprints (also called digital dossiers) include Internet activities such as social networking, email, chat rooms, cell phone text messages, phone calls, and photo/video messages. Students often think these are private communications, but in reality they are archived by cell phone companies and Internet resources (backed up by the servers). For example, if a student has Gmail, every email is archived by Google; if a student sends pictures to Flickr, every image is archived by Flickr's servers. Once a student sends a message or posts to the web from a cell phone, this can't be erased! It becomes part of the student's permanent record. To help students understand this concept, I recommend that they watch the movie *Digital Dossier* (www.youtube.com/watch?v=79IYZVYIVLA).

Everything sent via text message (pictures, videos, text, audio, etc.) is public. Although students think that every message, image, and video sent or received on their cell phones is private communication, in fact, it is public and archived by the cell phone companies. There are many examples in the media of people who have been caught doing something illegal or inappropriate via their text messaging or phone calling records. One high-profile example of cell phone texts being used in court to devastating effect is the case of Detroit Mayor Kwame Kilpatrick.

Students should know their plans. Although students may be aware of all the features of their cell phones (such as mobile Internet or text messaging), sometimes they do not know what they are being charged for using these features. Therefore, it is important that students take some time to get to know their plans and how many text messages they can send, whether they have mobile Internet (with or without extra charges), how many calling minutes a month they have, and so forth. One teacher in this book, Jimbo Lamb, recommends that students bring in a copy of their cell phone plans and recent bills to go over the specific details of what their cell phones can and cannot do. This would also be a good time to go over the survey.

Create a Social Contract (the Rules)

Once teachers have gone over mobile safety guidelines, it is important to sit down with the students and create a "social contract" for classroom rules and regulations concerning use of cell phones for learning. The students should be able to contribute to this rules agreement. Here are the steps:

1. Explain to the students that there should be some rules concerning how their cell phones will be used in the classroom, and students have an opportunity to be part of the rule-making process (the goal is to

have no more than five simple rules to follow and a consequence for noncompliance).

2. Students should be asked to brainstorm rules. During the brainstorm, students should be encouraged to support each rule with reasons why it should be implemented. For example, for "cell phones should be on vibrate at all times," students proposing the rule should explain why this is important. If they can't, ask for other students to help explain it.

3. Once there is a workable list of rules, students should be encouraged to narrow the list to about five rules. You may want to do this yourself. You could also use the analogy of a professional job where one is given a cell phone and a contract. You could ask students to imagine that they are being given a professional contract: Which "rules" do they think should be implemented in their classroom? Using this analogy may also help to eliminate some redundant or unnecessary rules.

4. Once the rules have been selected, students should be asked to brainstorm consequences for not following the rules. Once again, ask students to decide on the best option. You should let the students know that you will be adding these rules and consequences to a permission form that will be sent home for parents and students to sign. Following is an example of one set of classroom rules for cell phone use and consequences.

   - Cell phones must be off or on vibrate at all times.

   - Cell phones should be placed in the front of the room and off at the beginning of class (at the designated table in your numbered slot) and whenever they are not needed for instruction.

   - All messages or media sent from your phone during class must be related to the lesson or activity (reminding students that every message sent is documented by the cell phone company and the person/server receiving it).

   - If you are referencing someone else in class, you must have their (recorded verbal or written) approval before posting or publishing.

Permission Form

At this point, parents need to be included in the conversation. Chapters 1 and 2 have some examples of parent permission forms. Keep in mind that the permission letter should also include some suggestions for parents' involvement in cell phone safety practices with their children.

If possible, the letter should also invite parents to a cell phone safety and learning information night that the teacher and/or administrators hold at the school (see Figure 5.2). The information night should be a time when parents can learn about the activities that their children will be doing with cell phones, the rules and regulations around the use, the cell phone safety curriculum being taught, the consequences for inappropriate use, alternatives for students without cell phones, and how parents can get involved in the cell phone learning process.

Alternatives

Some students will not have cell phones, and some who do may not have enough text messages or calling minutes per month to use their own device in the class activities. Therefore, it is vital that the teacher consider the "have nots." Following are a few ideas on how to create multiple access points in a lesson plan.

- Select an online resource that couples with cell phones, but also has web-based options for uploading or sharing. For example, if you use Flickr to send pictures to and from cell phones to a private place online, students who do not have cell phones can still upload to Flickr via the web.

- Intentionally putting students in groups or pairs where the teacher knows that at least one of the group members has a cell phone that can be used for the project is a simple way to keep the students who do not have cell phones anonymous (because the teacher can say, "Someone in each group should take out their cell phone to use for this activity").

- Allow students to use your own cell phone.

- Use landlines (many web-based cell phone resources have toll-free calling numbers) for phone calling activities.

- Center activities for K–8 students where the teacher can use one cell phone with all the students during center time.

Figure 5.2 Sample permission form and invitation to information night

Dear Parents and Guardians,

We are starting a new project this year in our biology course. The students will be taking pictures of different biological species that they encounter in their everyday lives and posting on a private class website. To capture the species in the everyday lives of the students, I have given them the option of using their cell phones to take the pictures and send them to the class website. Although the students are not required to have a cell phone for the project, they are welcome to use their own if they choose to and if you allow them. In class, we will be discussing issues of cell phone safety and etiquette before starting the project. I will be using the ConnectSafely Guidelines for Cellphone Safety (www.connectsafely.org/safety-tips-and-advice.html). If you would like to participate in this conversation, please feel free to attend the class sessions on March 5th and 6th during any of the biology class periods:

8:00–9:00 a.m.

9:10–10:10 a.m.

2:10–3:10

In addition, I will be holding an information night about cell phone safety and the project on March 3rd at 7:00 p.m. I will go over the project in detail, show you how it works, and also answer any questions you may have about using cell phones in learning.

There is some research that supports the need for using student cell phones in learning, and teaching students how to properly use their cell phones can be a productive and important tool for their future professional growth. This will be discussed in detail at the information night as well as during the March 5th and 6th class sessions.

Finally, you are welcome to participate in this project! We are using a private space in a photo-sharing site called Flickr, where all the photos will be sent and eventually posted to a map at the exact location they were uncovered. You are welcome to take a picture of a biological species that you encounter, then send it to kolb@flickr.com along with a short text message on what you think the species is and the location of where you took the picture! Feel free to check the website each week to see the learning progress. Login: Kolbbiology Password: Biokid

I hope to see you in class and/or on the March 3rd information night. In the meantime if you have any questions or concerns do not hesitate to contact me at kolb@gmail.com or by phone 777–555–5777.

I give permission for my child to use their cell phone for this project:

_____   (parent signature)

Continued

Figure 5.2, *Continued*

> **Rules agreed on by students and teacher:**
>
> - Cell phones must be on vibrate at all times.
>
> - Cell phones should be placed in the front of the room at the beginning of class (at the designated table in your numbered slot) and whenever they are not needed for instruction.
>
> - All mobile messages or media sent from your phone during class must be related to the lesson or activity
>
> - If you are referencing someone else in class, you must have their (recorded verbal or written) approval before posting or publishing.
>
> **Consequences:**
>
> - The student will no longer be allowed to use the cell phone for learning activities until the student has proved that they are responsible enough to follow the rules.
>
> I will adhere to the classroom rules for cell phone use:
>
> _____ (student signature)
>
> Thank you
>
> *Liz Kolb*

- Allow students to use hardcopy options that they hand in to you, and you upload the work to the online resource. This is important because a few parents do not want their children using cell phones in any capacity.

Parent Information Night

The parent information night should begin with an overview of why you are using the student cell phones. The next step must be to describe the project(s) that will revolve around cell phone use, and any cost associated with the project and student cell phone use. For example, if you are using Poll Everywhere with students, you should let parents know that there will be no extra cost associated with Poll Everywhere, but that standard text message rates apply. Therefore, if their children do not have unlimited texting, the children should know how many they can send before being charged extra. At this point, the parents should be informed of the alternatives that the students have for completing the project without using cell phones. For example, students could use a computer to vote in Poll Everywhere, use a paper ballot, team up with another student who has a cell phone, or use the teacher's cell phone. This would be a good time to allow the parents to try a portion of the project (such as texting to the Poll Everywhere poll or recording an audio response with Google Voice or Yodio).

Next, the parents should be informed of any change in school cell phone policy as a result of the project(s). Also, the parents should know the rules for cell phone use during the project and the consequences for the students who do not follow the rules.

Parents should be invited to participate in the activity (within reason). If their child does not have a cell phone, they might want to allow their child to use a parent's cell phone and complete the project with their child as a homework assignment. The parent could subscribe to a text alert feed such as Pulse.to (http://pulse.to) or Celly (http://cel.ly), where they can receive updates about the project on their cell phones so they have a conversation starter with their children. Alternatively, the parents could post images and text messages to the class blog that relate to the topic the students are researching (for example, for biology students studying local flora and fauna, parents could also send or text in pictures and videos of discoveries that they made). Another example would be to allow parents to upload their child's final projects to their cell phones (such as a ringtone rap that their child created, or a wallpaper art collage).

Finally, parents should be allowed to ask questions. You should let parents know that they will be asked for feedback during and after the project. You should give parents multiple ways to provide feedback: email address, a text message number, a voicemail (Google Voice would be great for this), and an online anonymous survey (such as Google Form). The parents should sign the permission form (if they have not already).

Begin … Slowly!

Teachers who have used student cell phones in learning emphasize the importance of starting slowly. Although there are hundreds of exciting and easy-to-use resources that couple with cell phones, there is no need to get through all of them in the first lesson. You should pick a simple resource to use, become comfortable with the resource yourself, then introduce it to students. Often you can begin by assigning a cell phone activity for extra credit or optional homework. You should use the resource multiple times and get feedback from students on any issues or concerns they may have had. When you feel comfortable, bring that same resource into the classroom for a learning activity. Continue to use the resource until you are completely comfortable (sometimes this takes a few weeks, other times in could be a whole school year). Now, you may consider moving on to another resource.

Remind, Remind, Remind!

Continue to remind students of cell phone safety and appropriate use each time they use cell phones in the classroom. Keep in mind that rules and consequences that were developed in the social contract need to be enforced.

Feedback

Although the teacher has given parents a way to communicate with teachers and administrators during the project(s), some parents may not take the initiative to do this. Therefore it is important that during the project (no more than halfway through) you send an anonymous survey to parents to receive feedback. The feedback could also relate to the parents' general questions about cell phone safety and learning. You could use Google Forms to set up a survey or even create an open-ended poll in Poll Everywhere to get general feedback. Figure 5.3 is an example of a Google Form survey for parent feedback.

Of course, at the end of the project you should ask for some final feedback on the project and use of cell phones.

Figure 5.3 Example of Google Form survey

Cell Phone Project Feedback

Please know that this feedback is 100% anonymous. I would appreciate your honest feedback about the student's cell phone project thus far.

Have you spoken with your child about mobile safety since this project began? If yes, then how often?
- ○ Yes-everyday
- ○ Yes-one or two days a week
- ○ Yes-once
- ○ No
- ○ Other: [   ]

Has your child spoke with you about the cell phone project?
- ○ Yes
- ○ No
- ○ Other: [   ]

Do you think the cell phone project has given your child a new perspective on how cell phones can be used as learning tools?
- ○ YES! Definitely
- ○ Yes, somewhat
- ○ Not sure yet
- ○ I have not seen any change
- ○ Other: [   ]

Do you think your child has enjoyed the cell phone project?

	1	2	3	4	5	
Not at all	○	○	○	○	○	They LOVE it!

Have you had any concerns with the cell phone project?

[   ]

Has your child had any technical difficulties with the cell phone project (such as their phone not working with the web resource)?

[   ]

Do you have any questions about mobile safety or etiquette?

[   ]

Figure 5.3, *Continued*

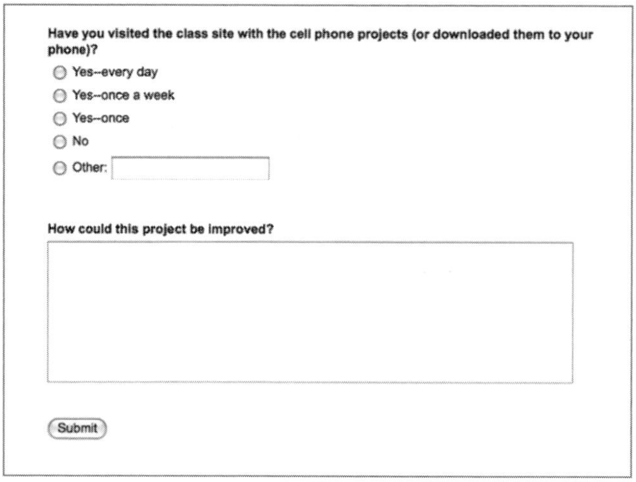

Have you visited the class site with the cell phone projects (or downloaded them to your phone)?

○ Yes--every day

○ Yes--once a week

○ Yes--once

○ No

○ Other: [   ]

How could this project be improved?

[   ]

(Submit)

Chapter 6

Web 2.0 Tools That Couple with Cell Phones

Chapter 4 covers a wide variety of web resources. This chapter includes many more web resources that work with cell phones and have not been mentioned previously in the book. Most of the following resources all have free options to couple with basic cell phones by audio, text, video, avatars, images, or a combination.

Audio

DialMyCalls

www.dialmycalls.com

DialMyCalls lets anyone tap into the power of sending voice messages out to entire phone lists in seconds. Through your Internet account on DialMyCalls, you can send your own voice messages from 2 to 200,000 phone numbers all within a few minutes.

Cinch

www.cinchcast.com

Cinch is a free and easy way to create and share audio, text, and photo updates using your phone or computer. Cinch enables you to capture and report on your experiences in a way that simple text just can't do. Using a simple interface, you can make and broadcast your content creations through Facebook, Twitter, and more.

GeoGraffiti

www.geograffiti.com

GeoGraffiti is a verbal billboard for sharing and retrieving voice messages to and from a specific location on a national map.

HistoryPhone

www.historyphone.net

HistoryPhone allows you to create professionally produced guided tours for museums, monuments, cities, and other sites of interest that can be heard via cell phone. Once your tour has been created, the user will just dial in, push one button, and the tour begins. Please note that there are charges for using HistoryPhone.

Phonevite

www.phonevite.com

Phonevite allows you to send free phone reminders and alerts to yourself and/or your friends in three quick, easy steps by entering your contact phone numbers, recording your message via your phone, and sending the message to all the numbers.

Rminder

http://core.rminder.com

Rminder provides an easy voice reminder service for your phone. You type in the text reminder on the website and it is converted to a voice reminder that is sent to your phone at the designated time and date.

Rondee

www.rondee.com

Rondee is a free conference calling service that offers a way to communicate with large groups over the phone. You can connect easily with any group on the phone with web-based scheduling, attendance tracking, record, and even a display of who's talking!

Text Messaging

myMemorizer

www.mymemorizer.com

myMemorizer is a reminder service where you add events or important dates, or subscribe to shared groups. myMemorizer will send a reminder as an email or as an SMS/text message to your cell phone.

Notify.Me

http://notify.me

Notify.me delivers website notifications that interest you in real time. For example, when new blog posts, news feeds, or items on eBay are posted, you will automatically receive a notification without having to check the website. Notifications are delivered to your destinations of choice such as instant messenger, cell phone, email, desktop, or web application.

Pulse.to

http://pulse.to

Pulse.to is similar to Celly (mentioned previously in this book). You can login to the website, create a free account and then set up "Pulses," which are public or private mass texting channels. In addition, you can control which users can send messages. Pulse.to works in many different countries besides the US and Canada. In addition there is not a shortcode to join, rather students/teachers/parents can text in to a real phone number (so phones that don't work with shortcodes or keywords will still work with this service). For example, to join my Pulse you would text JOIN KOLBY to 704-323-7775.

Remind101

http://remind101.com

This free service allows teachers to upload their syllabi and assignments to the Remind101 website. Students can then create accounts and set up text message reminders for all the due dates in their coursework.

Schoohoo

www.schoohoo.com

Schoohoo offers free school notifications and alerts to schools of any size. The web-based application allows schools to send alerts to parents, students, faculty, staff, even selected media—all via text message and email. Alerts can be sent about upcoming events such as early dismissals, school closings, emergencies, holidays, fundraising activities, and PTA meetings. The entire Schoohoo system is free of charge for schools and those receiving alerts—therefore, a short, 65-character text-only sponsor message is placed at the end of each alert.

SchoolTipline

www.schooltipline.com/en

SchoolTipline is a tool for anonymous feedback and information sharing in school communities. SchoolTipline provides administrators with an affordable and easy-to-use web-based service through which they can send and receive timely information and manage feedback from students, parents, and staff.

Studyboost

http://studyboost.com

You can create text-messaging flashcards with this free service. The teacher or students can set up flashcard reviews and students can subscribe via text message. Students can review their flashcard stacks at anytime from their phones!

Swaggle

http://swaggle.mobi

Similar to the Joopz application mentioned previously in this book, this site allows users to create private or public group text messages.

WeTxt

www.wetxt.com

Also similar to Joopz, WeTxt users can create groups to efficiently send text messages. WeTxt tracks all the messages sent from each account and allows for both public and private groups.

Wiggio

http://wiggio.com

Wiggio is set up for group communications and activities. On Wiggio, you can share and edit files, manage a group calendar, poll your group, post links, set up conference calls, chat online, and send mass text, voice, and email messages to your group members. Each group member can define how they want to be informed of group activity.

Zxing

http://zxing.appspot.com

Zxing is a free web-based QR (quick response) code generator. It works in a similar fashion to Kaywa (mentioned previously in the book). Anyone can submit a web address, image, email, or text and have it automatically generate into a QR code that can be printed or posted on the web.

Interactive Online Screens and Polling

Jumbli

http://jumbli.tv

Jumbli is a fun activity for literacy learning. You open the Jumbli screen and from the letters, just form a word and type it in. Then text your word to 40411.

LetsGoVote

www.letsgovote.com

This is similar to Poll Everywhere. Polls can be put into quiz form and results will be projected on an interactive web screen.

SMS Poll

www.smspoll.com

This works in a similar fashion to Poll Everywhere, except that it works in countries other than the United States.

Text the Mob

www.textthemob.com

This is also very similar to the Poll Everywhere application. Project polls or message boards on a large screen, have everyone send their input via their cell phones, and see results instantly!

Images and Video

Cellblock

http://cellblock.com

Share pictures and videos via email addresses and text message. Only the teacher needs to create an account, then students will be able to upload pictures and videos that instantly turn into a slideshow!

Flixwagon

http://flixwagon.com

Instantly broadcast live video to the Internet through your cell phone. Flixwagon works with most newer cell phones.

LiveCast

http://www.livecast.com

LiveCast can broadcast your video feed live from your cell phone to the Internet. It works with all smartphones.

Tumblr

www.tumblr.com

Tumblr lets you post text, photos, quotes, links, music, and videos to a personal website from your browser, phone, desktop, email, or wherever you happen to be.

Zannel

www.zannel.com

Group picture and video sharing from your phone.

Avatars

Beema

www.beema.com

This is similar to Voki, mentioned previously in this book. In Beema Animation, users choose a character from an extensive online collection of models and then record audio for the animation by placing a toll-free phone call in the U.S. or India, or using a microphone attached to a computer anywhere in the world. Beema then syncs the audio to the character and sends the new Beema back to the user via email. Beema will also deliver Beema Animation directly to a host of web services, including Twitter, YouTube, BlipTV, Treemo, Mocospace, and Blogger.

Mobile Quizzes and Surveys

Mobile Study

http://mobilestudy.org

Mobile Study allows anyone to create a quiz for cell phones. You can send the quiz via SMS text messaging or QR code to a phone (or iPod Touch).

Mobiode

http://mobiode.com

This web resource allows anyone to create a quiz or survey for cell phones. The quizzes and surveys can be taken via SMS text messaging or on a smartphone via the web. There is a cost for having more than one survey open at a time.

PK–5 students

PBS KIDS Mobile

http://pbskids.org/mobile

Download PBS KIDS games, podcasts, wallpapers, and ringtones you and your students can enjoy together on your mobile devices.

References

Bransford, J. D., Brown, A. L., & Cocking, R. R. (1999). *How people learn: Brain, mind, experience, and school.* Washington, DC: National Academies Press.

Brown, J. S., Collins, A., & Duguid, P. (1989). Situated cognition and the culture of learning. *Educational Researcher, 18*(1), 32–42.

Casner-Lotto, J., Barrington, L., Wright, M. (2006) *Are they really ready to work? Employers' perspectives on the basic knowledge and applied skills of new entrants to the 21st century U.S. workforce.* Retrieved from www.p21.org/documents/FINAL_REPORT_PDF09-29-06.pdf

Common Sense Media. (2009). *Hi-tech cheating: Cell phones and cheating in schools. A national poll.* Retrieved from www.commonsensemedia.org/hi-tech-cheating/

Coventry University. (2010). *Is texting valuable or vandalism?* Retrieved from wwwm.coventry.ac.uk/NewsCentre/pages/NewsArticle.aspx?ArticleId=120

CTIA—The Wireless Association. (2007). *U.S. wireless subscribership passes 250 million mark* [Press release]. Retrieved from www.ctia.org/media/press/body.cfm/prid/1724

Hancock, M., Randall, R., & Simpson, A. (2009, Summer). *From safety to literacy: Digital citizenship in the 21st century.* Threshold: A publication of Cable in the Classroom, 4–7.

Lee, C. (2003). Towards a framework for culturally responsive design in multimedia computer environments. *Mind, Culture, and Activity, 10*(1), 42–61.

Lemke, C., Coughlin, E., Thadani, V., & Martin, C. (2007). *EnGauge 21st century skills: Literacy in the digital age.* Retrieved from www.metiri.com/21/21%20Century%20Skills%20Final.doc

Lenhart, A. (2009). *Teens and sexting.* Retrieved from www.pewinternet.org/Reports/2009/Teens-and-Sexting.aspx

Minsky, M. (1988). *The society of mind.* New York: Simon & Schuster.

Moje, E. B., & Sutherland, L.M. (2003). The future of middle school literacy education. *English Education, 35*(2), 149–164.

Motlik, S. (2008). Mobile learning in developing nations. *International Review of Research in Open and Distance Learning, 9*(2), 1–7.

Ng'ambi, D. (2006). Collaborative questioning: A case of short message services (SMS) for knowledge sharing. In *Proceedings of the IEEE International Conference on Advanced Learning Technologies*. Kerkrade, Netherlands. 2–7 July. pp. 350–351.

Papert, S. (1980). *Mindstorms: Children, computers and powerful ideas*. New York, NY: Basic Books.

Partnership for 21st Century Skills. (2007). *Beyond the three Rs: Voter attitudes toward 21st century skills*. Retrieved from www.21stcenturyskills.org/documents/P21_pollreport_singlepg.pdf

Project Tomorrow. (2008, April 8). *Speak Up 2007 for Students, Teachers, Parents & School Leaders selected national findings*. Retrieved from www.tomorrow.org/speakup/speakup_reports.html

Project Tomorrow. (2008, July 1). *Learning in the 21st century: A trends update—key findings from Speak Up 2007 survey* [PowerPoint slides]. Retrieved from www.tomorrow.org/speakup/learning21Report_Update.html

Rainie, L. (2006, March 23). *Life online: Teens and technology and the world to come*. Retrieved from www.pewInternet.org/PPF/r/63/presentation_display.asp

Reid, D. J., & Reid, F. (2004). *Insights into the social and psychological effects of text messaging*. University of Plymouth. Retrieved from www.160characters.org/documents/SocialEffectsOfTextMessaging.pdf

Richardson, V. (1996). The role of attitudes and beliefs in learning to teach. In Sikula, J., Buttery, T., & Guyton, E. (Eds.), *Handbook of research on teacher education* (2nd ed., pp. 102–119). New York, NY: Macmillan.

Slate—Slates in schools. (n.d.). Retrieved from www.llechicymru.info/slatesinschools.english.htm

Smith, A. (2009, April 15). The Internet's role in Campaign 2008. Retrieved from www.pewInternet.org/Reports/2009/6--The-Internets-Role-in-Campaign-2008.aspx

Speak Up 2009. (2010). *Creating our future: Students speak up about their vision for 21st century learning*. Retrieved from www.tomorrow.org/speakup/pdfs/SU09NationalFindingsStudents&Parents.pdf

Transition brief: Policy recommendations on preparing Americans for the global skills race. (2008). Paper prepared for the Partnership for 21st Century Skills. Retrieved from www.p21.org/documents/p21_transition_paper_nov_24_2008.pdf.

Webopedia. (2011). Digital footprint. Retrieved from www.webopedia.com/TERM/D/digital_footprint.html

National Educational Technology Standards for Students (NETS•S)

All K–12 students should be prepared to meet the following standards and performance indicators.

1. Creativity and Innovation

Students demonstrate creative thinking, construct knowledge, and develop innovative products and processes using technology. Students:

a. apply existing knowledge to generate new ideas, products, or processes

b. create original works as a means of personal or group expression

c. use models and simulations to explore complex systems and issues

d. identify trends and forecast possibilities

2. Communication and Collaboration

Students use digital media and environments to communicate and work collaboratively, including at a distance, to support individual learning and contribute to the learning of others. Students:

a. interact, collaborate, and publish with peers, experts, or others employing a variety of digital environments and media

b. communicate information and ideas effectively to multiple audiences using a variety of media and formats

c. develop cultural understanding and global awareness by engaging with learners of other cultures

d. contribute to project teams to produce original works or solve problems

3. Research and Information Fluency

Students apply digital tools to gather, evaluate, and use information. Students:

a. plan strategies to guide inquiry

b. locate, organize, analyze, evaluate, synthesize, and ethically use information from a variety of sources and media

c. evaluate and select information sources and digital tools based on the appropriateness to specific tasks

d. process data and report results

4. Critical Thinking, Problem Solving, and Decision Making

Students use critical-thinking skills to plan and conduct research, manage projects, solve problems, and make informed decisions using appropriate digital tools and resources. Students:

a. identify and define authentic problems and significant questions for investigation

b. plan and manage activities to develop a solution or complete a project

c. collect and analyze data to identify solutions and make informed decisions

d. use multiple processes and diverse perspectives to explore alternative solutions

5. Digital Citizenship

Students understand human, cultural, and societal issues related to technology and practice legal and ethical behavior. Students:

a. advocate and practice the safe, legal, and responsible use of information and technology

b. exhibit a positive attitude toward using technology that supports collaboration, learning, and productivity

c. demonstrate personal responsibility for lifelong learning

d. exhibit leadership for digital citizenship

6. Technology Operations and Concepts

Students demonstrate a sound understanding of technology concepts, systems, and operations. Students:

    a. understand and use technology systems

    b. select and use applications effectively and productively

    c. troubleshoot systems and applications

    d. transfer current knowledge to the learning of new technologies

National Educational Technology Standards for Teachers (NETS•T)

All classroom teachers should be prepared to meet the following standards and performance indicators.

1. Facilitate and Inspire Student Learning and Creativity

Teachers use their knowledge of subject matter, teaching and learning, and technology to facilitate experiences that advance student learning, creativity, and innovation in both face-to-face and virtual environments. Teachers:

    a. promote, support, and model creative and innovative thinking and inventiveness

    b. engage students in exploring real-world issues and solving authentic problems using digital tools and resources

    c. promote student reflection using collaborative tools to reveal and clarify students' conceptual understanding and thinking, planning, and creative processes

    d. model collaborative knowledge construction by engaging in learning with students, colleagues, and others in face-to-face and virtual environments

2. Design and Develop Digital-Age Learning Experiences and Assessments

Teachers design, develop, and evaluate authentic learning experiences and assessments incorporating contemporary tools and resources to maximize content learning in context and to develop the knowledge, skills, and attitudes identified in the NETS•S. Teachers:

    a. design or adapt relevant learning experiences that incorporate digital tools and resources to promote student learning and creativity

Cell Phones in the Classroom ▪ A Practical Guide for Educators

b. develop technology-enriched learning environments that enable all students to pursue their individual curiosities and become active participants in setting their own educational goals, managing their own learning, and assessing their own progress

c. customize and personalize learning activities to address students' diverse learning styles, working strategies, and abilities using digital tools and resources

d. provide students with multiple and varied formative and summative assessments aligned with content and technology standards and use resulting data to inform learning and teaching

3. Model Digital-Age Work and Learning

Teachers exhibit knowledge, skills, and work processes representative of an innovative professional in a global and digital society. Teachers:

a. demonstrate fluency in technology systems and the transfer of current knowledge to new technologies and situations

b. collaborate with students, peers, parents, and community members using digital tools and resources to support student success and innovation

c. communicate relevant information and ideas effectively to students, parents, and peers using a variety of digital-age media and formats

d. model and facilitate effective use of current and emerging digital tools to locate, analyze, evaluate, and use information resources to support research and learning

4. Promote and Model Digital Citizenship and Responsibility

Teachers understand local and global societal issues and responsibilities in an evolving digital culture and exhibit legal and ethical behavior in their professional practices. Teachers:

a. advocate, model, and teach safe, legal, and ethical use of digital information and technology, including respect for copyright, intellectual property, and the appropriate documentation of sources

   b. address the diverse needs of all learners by using learner-centered strategies and providing equitable access to appropriate digital tools and resources

   c. promote and model digital etiquette and responsible social interactions related to the use of technology and information

   d. develop and model cultural understanding and global awareness by engaging with colleagues and students of other cultures using digital-age communication and collaboration tools

5. Engage in Professional Growth and Leadership

Teachers continuously improve their professional practice, model lifelong learning, and exhibit leadership in their school and professional community by promoting and demonstrating the effective use of digital tools and resources. Teachers:

   a. participate in local and global learning communities to explore creative applications of technology to improve student learning

   b. exhibit leadership by demonstrating a vision of technology infusion, participating in shared decision making and community building, and developing the leadership and technology skills of others

   c. evaluate and reflect on current research and professional practice on a regular basis to make effective use of existing and emerging digital tools and resources in support of student learning

   d. contribute to the effectiveness, vitality, and self-renewal of the teaching profession and of their school and community